LES PRESIDENTS DES ETATS-UNIS.

LES PRESIDENTS DES ETATS-UNIS.

VOLUME

2

THE
AMERICAN HERITAGE
BOOK OF THE
PRESIDENTS
AND FAMOUS AMERICANS

★ ★ ★ ★ ★

THOMAS JEFFERSON

JAMES MADISON

JAMES MONROE

CREATED AND DESIGNED BY THE EDITORS OF
AMERICAN HERITAGE
The Magazine of History

12-VOLUME EDITION PUBLISHED BY
DELL PUBLISHING CO., INC., NEW YORK, N.Y.

THE WHITE HOUSE COLLECTION

Thomas Jefferson

COLONIAL WILLIAMSBURG

— COURTESY OF NATIONAL PORTRAIT GALLERY, SMITHSONIAN INSTITUTION

James Madison

James Monroe

CONTENTS
OF VOLUME TWO

FAMOUS AMERICANS

THE THIRD PRESIDENT (1801–1809)

THOMAS JEFFERSON

Near the foot of the road that leads up to Monticello, a granite obelisk, visible through the gates of a graveyard, bears these words: "Here was buried Thomas Jefferson, author of the Declaration of American Independence, of the Statute of Virginia for Religious Freedom, and father of the University of Virginia."

This epitaph, composed by Jefferson himself, was modest for a man who had also served as minister to France, governor of Virginia, the first Secretary of State, the second Vice President, and—for two remarkable terms—the third President of the United States.

Perhaps Jefferson knew that history would read and write carefully between his lines. And it did. "The principles of Jefferson," Abraham Lincoln would say, "are the definitions and axioms of a free society." To other admirers he would become "a man of steel clothed in homespun" and "the Apostle of Americanism." To his detractors and enemies, however, he was less than anointed: "a howling atheist," an agent of Napoleon, a lecher, worshiping "some infamous prostitute, under the title of the Goddess of Reason." Alexander Hamilton derided Jefferson's "womanish attachment to France," and was convinced that his disinterest and republicanism actually concealed a thirst for power.

Admiration and attack notwithstanding, the range of Jefferson's interests and skills was almost incredible. Pre-eminently a statesman and politician, he was also an adept writer, lawyer, farmer, naturalist, architect, musician, linguist, classicist, philosopher, scientist, geographer, surveyor, botanist, ethnologist, and paleontologist. He was interested in everything, from the origin of the rainbow to the habitat of the wild turkey, from fossils and Newtonian physics to calculus, Anglo-Saxon grammar, and the condition of Negroes in

Thomas Jefferson, painted by Rembrandt Peale in 1805

95

Santo Domingo. Books, he said, were the "greatest of all amusements." He read Cicero in Latin, Plato in Greek, Montesquieu in French, Cervantes in Spanish. To fathom the poet Ossian, he studied Gaelic. He compiled Indian vocabularies. And even on a backbreaking, three-mile-an-hour, ten-day stagecoach trip from Williamsburg to Philadelphia in 1775, he made notes on fauna and flora and odd coins. As a naturalist, he recorded the growth of trees and flowers, the appearance of birds, the advance and recess of frost. As an inventive farmer, he introduced the moldboard plow to the American Philosophical Society, which he headed from 1796 to 1815. A connoisseur of art, he had one of the finest collections of sculpture and paintings in America.

For all his activities, however, Jefferson was essentially a home-centered, contemplative man. Wherever he was—in France or Philadelphia, among scholars or kings—he was always eager to return to Monticello. "But the enormities of the times in which I have lived," he said in 1809, "have forced me to take a part in resisting them, and to commit myself on the boisterous ocean of political passions."

Jefferson's departure from his "country" (as he always called Virginia) to make his entrance into politics was no less than epochal for the United States. "Jefferson's was to be the leading mind of the first age of our national life," historian Daniel Boorstin concludes, "and therefore in a powerful position for shaping the American intellectual character."

Thomas Jefferson was born, one of ten children, on April 13, 1743, midway through the reign of George II. His birthplace was "Shadwell" in Goochland (now Albemarle) County on Virginia's western frontier. His parents were Peter Jefferson, a prosperous tobacco plantation owner and surveyor, and Jane (Randolph) Jefferson, daughter of one of Virginia's first families, descended from English and Scottish nobility, "to which," Jefferson would wryly add in old age, "let everyone ascribe the . . . merit he chooses."

Thomas' early education was entrusted to the Reverend Mr. William Douglas, for whom Jefferson appears to have had little regard, but from whom he acquired the rudiments of Latin, Greek, and French. When Peter Jefferson died in 1757, Thomas left Douglas' tutelage and studied for two years in a log cabin classroom under the iconoclastic Reverend Mr. James Maury, whom Jefferson described as a "correct classical scholar," and under whose guidance he mastered several languages and was introduced to natural philosophy and geology.

On January 14, 1760, Jefferson wrote a decisive letter to his guardian, Colonel John Harvie, in which he asked for permission to attend William and Mary in Williamsburg. "By going to the College," he reasoned, "I shall get a more universal Acquaintance, which may hereafter be serviceable to me; & I suppose I can pursue my studies in the Greek & Latin as well there as here, & likewise learn something of the Mathematics." Jefferson left the frontier for Williamsburg in March, 1760, and enrolled at the college. The gay capital of colonial Virginia must have been an abrupt change for the provincial student, who nursed at least one hangover from an Apollo Tavern carouse. "I never could have thought," he recorded for posterity on that occasion, "the succeeding

The College of William and Mary is shown at left as it looked in colonial times. It was the second oldest college in the colonies, having opened in 1694, fifty-eight years after the establishment of Harvard. The structures are, from left to right, Brafferton Hall, which housed Indian students, the Wren, or main, building, and the home of the school's president.

sun would have seen me so wretched as I now am!"

Sensitive, shy, and soft spoken, Jefferson was "Long Tom," well over six feet tall, slender, broad-shouldered, his jaw set square, his hands large, his limbs disproportionately long. A gangling, freckled, hazel-eyed redhead, he was a sloucher and a lounger. But his brilliant mind brought him to the attention of the intellectuals of Williamsburg, including his mentor at the college, Dr. William Small, professor of mathematics, natural history, and moral philosophy.

Jefferson graduated from William and Mary in April, 1762, and became an apprentice in the Williamsburg office of George Wythe, one of Virginia's leading jurists. Wythe joined Small in introducing the promising scholar to Virginia's royal governor, Francis Fauquier, at whose table this improbable threesome would often be honored at dinner, where the discussion of politics, literature, music, and philosophy was easily the main course. Though unimpressed by the argot of law, Jefferson was admitted to the bar of the General Court in 1767. He did well as a lawyer, numbering among his clients such prominent Virginia families as the Randolphs, Pendletons, and Pages.

On January 1, 1772, Jefferson married a well-to-do widow, Martha (Wayles) Skelton, in the Anglican rite. He was twenty-eight, she twenty-three. Martha, or Patty, as Jefferson called her, was beautiful, graceful, and high-spirited. A year after the marriage, her father died, leaving her 40,000 acres of land and 135 slaves. But she also inherited a large debt, which accounted in part for Jefferson's subsequent financial troubles.

Moving into the still uncompleted Monticello (construction had begun in 1769), the newlyweds were at first restricted to Jefferson's one-room bachelor quarters. Martha Jefferson was to bear Thomas six children, of whom only Martha ("Patsy") and Maria ("Polly") lived to maturity. Throughout her marriage, Mrs. Jefferson was wracked by chronic miscarriages, contributing to her ill health and to her early death at thirty-three.

In December, 1768, Jefferson had been elected to the Virginia House of Burgesses; he retained his seat there until the royal dissolution of the House in 1775. One of his first acts as a legislator was to introduce, unsuccessfully, a bill to permit owners to free their slaves. Jefferson also held the posts of Albemarle County lieutenant (1770) and Albemarle County surveyor (1773). While not an outstanding public speaker, he excelled as a committeeman and was recognized early as an accomplished writer.

On March 12, 1773, Jefferson and other members of Virginia's radical, anti-British group drew up resolves creating the Virginia Committee of Correspondence to maintain secret contact with the North. The closing of the port of Boston in 1774 resulted in a resolution to side with the Northern rebels; Jefferson championed proclamation of a symbolic fast day to protest the British tyranny in Massachusetts. When the governor of Virginia, the Earl of Dunmore, dissolved the House of Burgesses, Jefferson and his fellow rebels met on May 27, 1774, at the Raleigh Tavern, declaring that "an attack on any one colony should be considered as an attack on the whole." They also agreed that Virginia's counties should elect delegates to a convention that would select representatives

97

At this portable writing desk Jefferson composed the first draft of the Declaration of Independence.

to the Continental Congress. Albemarle County chose Jefferson as its delegate to the Virginia convention, but dysentery prevented him from attending. He drafted, however, an eloquent protest against royal policy: *A Summary View of the Rights of British America*. It was rejected by the Virginians as too bold, but it made Jefferson a major spokesman for republican America.

Addressed directly to George III, *A Summary View* is a classic of political advocacy and polemic. Jefferson's case for colonial grievances against the Crown was based not merely on evident commercial and political injustice, but also on the natural rights of Englishmen themselves—inherent and irrevocable rights that the King would not have dared to contravene in his own country. "Kings," he reminded George, "are the servants, not the proprietors of the people." Denying all parliamentary authority over the American states, Jefferson informed the sovereign that the colonies' initial submission to him had been voluntary, clearly implying that what had been freely given could also, in tyranny, be withdrawn.

Demanding freedom of world trade in goods that Britain could not use, and an end to taxation of a people not represented in London, Jefferson ridiculed the idea that 160,000 electors in Britain should tyrannize America's four million people through a capricious Parliament, subject, in colonial matters, to the whims and delays of a callous King. Special trade privileges for Britain were acceptable, said Jefferson, still hoping for conciliation, but despotic rule was not.

A Summary View hit the colonies—and Europe—with tremendous force. Jefferson was promptly proscribed by Parliament in a bill of attainder, still another British violation of British law.

In the summer of 1775, he was elected to serve as alternate to Peyton Randolph, a Virginia delegate at the Second Continental Congress. By this time, the fighting at Lexington was history. "This accident," Jefferson said, "has cut off any hope of reconciliation." At the Congress, Jefferson made no speeches, but served on two committees.

Because both his wife and daughter were ill, Jefferson left for Monticello in December of 1775. He found Virginia enraged by Lord Dunmore's punitive burning of Norfolk in January, 1776. Saddened by the death of his mother and suffering from migraine headaches, Jefferson did not return to Philadelphia until May. Less than one month later, on June 7, Virginia's Richard Henry Lee rose to propose a resolution that would change forever the course of human history. Be it resolved, Lee declared, "That these United Colonies are and of right ought to be free and independent states, that they are absolved from all allegiance to the British crown, and that all political connection between them and the state of Great Britain is and ought to be, totally dissolved."

Congress, delaying its vote on the Lee resolution until July 1, appointed a committee of five to draft a formal Declaration of Independence: Thomas Jefferson of Virginia, John Adams of Massachusetts, Benjamin Franklin of Pennsylvania, Roger Sherman of Connecticut, and Robert R. Livingston of New York. The committee, deferring to the thirty-three-year-old Jefferson's established skill as a writer and advocate (he had just written the preamble to the Virginia constitution), delegated him to draft the Declaration. From June 11 to June 28 he worked on it, polishing, changing, rewriting. After amendments by Adams and Franklin were incorporated, the committee submitted the document to the Congress on June 28, 1776.

Jefferson's original draft contained more than 1,800 words. Congress expunged 460, including a stunning condemnation of slavery, as Long Tom sat mute and hurt, and the redoubtable Adams defended the document, word by word. Approved by Congress on July 2, the Declaration was issued to the nation and the world on July 4, 1776.

The Declaration did not merely express American thought; it changed it, inspired it, and committed it to the principle of freedom for all men. Expressing the eighteenth century's faith in human reason and contempt for unearned authority, the document rang with optimism, with the equation of desire and achievement. Jefferson wrote as if tyranny had never been truly binding, as if man had just been born and was building his first house of government. As in *A Summary View*, he carefully catalogued the King's "long train of abuses and usurpations": his legislative, commercial, and judicial despotism; his absentee bureaucracy; his naval depredations; his onerous mercantile taxes; his incitement of American Indians against the colonists; his most unprincely and unchristian conduct.

But the Declaration was—and remains—epochal, not merely as a formal document of rebellion by one specific nation against another. Its greatness lies in its soaring affirmation of unassailable human liberty. Men were to be free, Jefferson wrote, not merely because they wanted to, or because tyranny was intrinsically unjust. Men were to be free because they were, in fact, free under "the laws of nature and of nature's God." Human rights were not magnanimously granted by monarchs and therefore retractable. Human rights were an indissoluble birthright given by God and therefore inalienable. And first among these were the rights of "life, liberty, and the pursuit of happiness." Government's only just function was to secure and advance these rights; when a government ceased to perform this function, it was the duty of men to rebel against it and form another.

Accordingly, America now declared itself thirteen "free and independent states . . . absolved from all allegiance to the British crown." Accordingly, too, America stated the creed of liberty by which it would judge events, and *be* judged for ages to come.

His major task completed, Jefferson remained in Congress for the first debates on the Articles of Confederation, and then left for Monticello in September of 1776. There was, after all, much Revolutionary work to be done at home in Virginia. On October 7, Jefferson entered the Old Dominion's newly designated House of Delegates, where he remained until 1779. In the House, Jefferson spearheaded prodigious legislative achievements. Of one hundred and twenty-six reform bills he sired, at least one hundred

A Declaration by the Representatives of the UNITED STATES OF AMERICA, in General Congress assembled.

When in the course of human events it becomes necessary for one people to dissolve the political bands which have connected them with another, and to assume among the powers of the earth the separate and equal station to which the laws of nature & of nature's god entitle them, a decent respect to the opinions of mankind requires that they should declare the causes which impel them to the separation.

Above is Jefferson's rough manuscript of words that subsequent generations would learn by heart at school.

passed. The law of primogeniture and entails was abolished. The criminal law was revised. Although his bill to establish a system of general education failed to pass, it remained a model for future laws.

In 1779, Jefferson introduced the Act for Establishing Religious Freedom, which was not, however, adopted until 1786. This classic bill guaranteed that "no man shall be compelled to frequent or support any religious worship, place, or ministry whatsoever," and that "all men shall be free to profess, and by argument to maintain, their opinions in matters of religion, and that the same shall in nowise diminish, enlarge, or affect their civil capacities." Jefferson reasoned that "our civil rights have no dependence on our religious opinions, more than our opinions in physics or geometry," and that official attempts to impose an established state religion breed only hypocrisy and corruption of the very faith they purport to espouse. Although not a churchgoer himself, Jefferson was, nonetheless, deeply religious. He described himself as "a real Christian," subscribing to the ethics of Jesus, if not the metaphysics of Christianity.

On June 1, 1779, Jefferson succeeded Patrick Henry as wartime governor. From the start, his administration was beset by ills. Objectively, Jefferson was plagued by an inadequate militia and by border harassments by Indians. Fear of an impending British invasion, for which Virginians were unprepared, pervaded the state. Subjectively, Jefferson was less effective as an executive than as a seer, committeeman, and draftsman. He eschewed, even in war, the use of illegal or arbitrary executive means toward just ends. When Britain finally invaded Virginia in force, he resigned, urging his replacement by a military governor, and retired to Monticello. On June 4, 1781, the British pursued him to Monticello, and he fled to Poplar Forest, a cottage one hundred miles away.

An angered House of Delegates, after electing Thomas Nelson, Jr. military governor, ordered an inquiry into Jefferson's conduct as governor and his failure to organize an adequate militia. A more clement House, in December, 1781, absolved Jefferson of guilt.

On September 6, 1782, Jefferson's wife died. Although he had been determined never to return to politics, the loneliness of his mansion now caused him "to seek relief from personal woe in public activity." In June of 1783, he was elected a delegate to the Continental Congress, where his legislative proposals were formidable. He suggested the adoption of a national dollar, subdivided into tenths and hundredths—a measure approved during Washington's administration with the concurrence of Alexander Hamilton. His Report of Government for the Western Territory (core of the later Ordinance of 1787) advocated the exclusion of slavery in all Western territories after 1800. He also drew up a schema for the final peace treaty with Great Britain, and a report that would establish procedure in the drafting of commercial agreements.

In May, 1784, Jefferson was appointed to assist Franklin and Adams in Europe in the preparation of consular treaties. A year later, he was named Franklin's successor as minister to France, a post he held until October of 1789. Franklin's homespun wit and forthrightness had won the heart of Paris, but

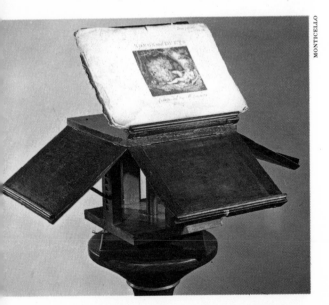

MONTICELLO

Among Thomas Jefferson's many inventions for his household was the revolving music stand above.

Jefferson's beloved daughter "Patsy" is shown here as she looked around 1786, when she was in Paris.

Jefferson evaded comparisons, adroitly insisting that he had come not to replace Franklin, only to succeed him. As minister, Jefferson presented America's revolutionary case with erudition and dexterity, hailed France tactfully as a counterpoise to a common British antagonist, and negotiated a consular convention.

"On France itself," Nathan Schachner writes, "Jefferson was of two minds. He envied the French their architecture, sculpture, painting, and music; but nothing else. Fresh from the spaciousness of America, where institutions, no matter how far behind the ideal, at least were liberal and progressive, where the people walked with an independent air and poverty was practically unknown, the swarming alleys of Paris, the contrast between resplendent Court and the hopeless masses . . . filled him with a sense of horror." To see the world, Jefferson would say, is to love America all the more.

In a sense, Jefferson never really left home; his eye was ever on Virginia. While in France, he designed the buildings for the new state capital at Richmond, worked on plans for his beloved Monticello, and heard the glad news that his Act for Establishing Religious Freedom had passed the Virginia legislature in 1786. From Paris, too, reviewing the newly adopted Constitution by mail with his friend James Madison, he insisted on the prompt inclusion of a bill of rights.

Despite official United States neutrality in France's revolution, Jefferson was patently sympathetic with the more moderate revolutionists, who were at once the source of his diplomatic data and contacts and the object of his special concern. He proposed to the Marquis de Lafayette a new charter for France, and to Lafayette's aunt, Madame de Tessé, a procedural form for the French Assembly of Notables. In later years Jefferson would maintain that every cultivated and traveled man would prefer France as a principal alternative to his own country.

Still, Jefferson was glad to start for home in October, 1789, to return to family, farm, and books. As he approached Monticello, two days before Christmas, his servants spotted his phaeton and followed it up the steep hill to the mansion. "When the door of the carriage was opened," his daughter Martha recorded, "they received him in their arms and bore him to the house, crowding round and kissing his hands and feet, some blubbering and crying, others laughing. It seemed impossible to satisfy their anxiety to touch and kiss the very earth which bore him."

On his return from Europe, Jefferson's basic philosophy, modified at least marginally by the French revolutionary experience, was already clear. He had, above all, a confirmed and unsullied faith in America, viewing it in candent Biblical terms as a promised land. But America's abundance and promise, Jefferson argued in 1789, was no cause for pride. The United States, he said, must "show by example the sufficiency of human reason for the care of human affairs and that the will of the majority, the Natural Law of every society, is the only sure guardian of the rights of man."

Impressed by the ideology of the Enlightenment, Jefferson shared its faith in reason, science, and human perfectibility. "We believed," he would say in retrospect in 1823, "that man was a rational animal, endowed by nature with rights and with an innate sense of justice . . . that he could be restrained from wrong and protected in right, by moderate powers confided to persons of his own choice, and held to their duties by dependence on his own will." He believed also in the superiority of agrarian virtue, unsullied by industry and commerce. "Those who labor in the earth," Jefferson had said in his *Notes on Virginia*, "are the chosen people of God. . . ." Urging American reliance on the products of Europe, already hopelessly corrupted by factories, he turned with contempt on the urban community: "The mobs of great cities add just so much to the support of pure government, as sores do to the strength of the human body."

Bacon, Newton, and Locke were for Jefferson a "trinity of the three greatest men the world had ever produced." He admired Bacon for his theory of inductive reasoning from observed fact, for his theory of movement from clinically measurable data to hypothesis, experiment, and control. He valued Newton for his revolutionary description of a physical world governed by predictable laws of cause and effect, applicable no less to human conduct than to the elements. Locke became his fountainhead for his concept of natural human rights, founded not on the will of man but in the very substance of the natural order, rights discoverable to human reason. He admired, too, Locke's belief that man protected his natural rights to life, liberty, and property in voluntary mutual contract, organizing a protective government, desirable and sufferable only if its selected leaders lived up to its terms.

Appointed by Washington in December, 1789, as the first Secretary of State, Jefferson arrived in New York to assume his duties in March of the following year. It was a difficult tenure. Although he collaborated with Hamilton on the federal government's assumption of state debts, in exchange for Hamilton's concession that the new national capital be located on the banks of the Potomac, he was distressed to see Washington espouse Hamilton's plan for a central Bank of the United States—to Jefferson an insidious concentration of wealth. As an agrarian, he regarded banks as parasitic.

Unhappy over Hamilton's leading role in the administration, Jefferson asked to retire by the end of 1792. He was persuaded by the President to stay on at least another year to avoid overt Federalist-Republican dissension within the government. During this period, his coinage and monetary system was adopted with Hamilton's approval, and Jefferson had to deal with a major political problem—the French appointment of Citizen Edmond Genêt as minister to the United States. Jefferson said in 1793 that rather than see the French Revolution fail he "would . . . have seen half the earth desolated." But when Genêt, despite America's officially stated neutrality in the Franco-British conflict, "spoke of going over President Washington's head" in direct appeal to the American people for assistance against England, Jefferson was nonplused. He recommended Genêt's prompt expulsion.

Disappointed by France and still frustrated by Hamilton, Jefferson was now determined to resign and held Washington to his promise to let him go at the end of 1793. On January 16, 1794, Jefferson was back at Monticello. His retirement would be brief, however. In 1796, the Republicans, incensed by the reign of wealth and privilege and by Jay's Treaty, nominated Jefferson and Aaron Burr to oppose John Adams in his bid for the Presidency. Jefferson lost the election to Adams by three electoral votes, thus becoming Vice President for four more years of Federalist frustration.

Republican sentiment against the Federalists became frenetic with the passage of the Alien and Sedition Acts, which they viewed as an odious attempt to silence or intimidate all opposition. "Against us," Jefferson wrote, "are . . . all the officers of the government, all who want to be officers, all timid men who prefer the calm of despotism to the boisterous sea of liberty. . . ." Now

Jefferson abandoned all semblance of impartiality and plunged into overt leadership of the emerging Republican party. The Alien and Sedition Acts, he told Madison in June of 1800, were "so palpably in the teeth of the Constitution as to show they [the Federalists] mean to pay no respect to it."

To counter the federal government and reassert the states' rights to political freedom, Jefferson pushed through the Kentucky legislature (and Madison through Virginia's) a series of resolutions declaring the Alien and Sedition Acts unconstitutional. In Kentucky, Jefferson argued a primary brief of the Southern case. "Where powers are assumed which have not been delegated," he said, "a nullification of the act is the rightful remedy."

In 1800, Jefferson was nominated by the Republicans for the Presidency of the United States. His running mate was Aaron Burr; his opponents, John Adams, seeking re-election, and Charles Pinckney. Jefferson's basic concept of the federal role, as he approached the election, was presented in a lucid letter of 1799 to Elbridge Gerry. "I am for preserving to the States," he wrote, "the powers not yielded by them to the Union. . . . I am not for transferring all the powers of the States to the General Government, and all those of that government to the executive branch." He said he preferred "a government rigorously frugal and simple," its savings promptly applied to discharging the national debt, its attitude firmly fixed against bureaucracy based on spoils. Dismissing a standing army as a coercive menace to liberty, and urging a navy limited to coastal patrol, he advocated a strong militia as adequate to maintaining the social order, short of invasion. He urged free trade with all.

Despite five years of ministry in France, Jefferson advocated "little or no diplomatic establishment" and opposed foreign alliances. In another assault on the Alien and Sedition Acts, he declared himself "against all violations of the Constitution to silence by force and not by reason the complaints or criticisms, just or unjust, of our citizens

This 1800 cartoon attacked Jefferson for his letter to Philip Mazzei, an Italian friend, in which he violently accused the Federalists of despotism.

against the conduct of their agents." In light of Jefferson's conduct as President, these statements take on ironic significance: although he did cut the American diplomatic corps to the bone, he was to reverse or abridge all the rest of these principles.

But now he faced a vicious campaign, a toxic stew of license and spleen. The Federalists were badly split, Hamilton openly warring with Adams. Hamilton raged against Jefferson, determined to prevent that "atheist in religion, and a fanatic in politics, from getting possession of the helm of state." It was a newspaper and pamphlet war, too, waged pre-eminently by Philip Freneau's Jeffersonian *National Gazette* and John Fenno's Hamiltonian *U.S. Gazette*. Jefferson was attacked as a drunkard, the father of numerous mulattoes, and an atheist. "Our churches will be prostrated," cried the *New-England Palladium*. "There is scarcely a possibility," added the *Connecticut Courant*,

AARON BURR

Aaron Burr possessed the brilliance, wit, and charm of a born leader. But he was an egomaniac who forever sowed the seeds of his own failure. Rising rapidly in the New York State Republican party, he received thirty electoral votes in the presidential election of 1796. Named as Jefferson's running mate four years later, he campaigned vigorously in New York and was largely responsible for the Republican victory. But when the electoral count showed him tied with Jefferson, his ambition overrode his common sense, and he declined to remove himself from competition, thus earning Jefferson's lasting distrust. Having failed to win the President's support for a second term as Vice President, and having lost his state's gubernatorial election, an embittered Burr challenged Alexander Hamilton to a duel and killed him. He then became involved in a scheme apparently aimed at separating at least part of the West from the United States, and conquering Mexico. Blinded by dreams of glory, he raised an army, but it was pitifully small, and he was arrested before he could do any damage. Charged with treason, Burr was brought to trial before Chief Justice John Marshall in 1807. Jefferson demanded a verdict of guilty, but the anti-Jefferson Chief Justice conducted the trial in a manner that led to Burr's acquittal. Burr then left for Europe, where he continued his intrigues fruitlessly. He died in New York in 1836.

"that we shall escape a *Civil War*. . . . Murder, robbery, rape, adultery, and incest will be openly taught and practiced. . . ."

While there was a definite understanding that Jefferson was running for the Presidency and Burr for the Vice Presidency, the method of voting demanded that state electors cast votes for two men, without distinguishing between their choices for the first and second offices. When Jefferson and Burr received the same number of votes, the election was thus thrust into a seething Federalist-controlled House of Representatives. The tie was not broken until thirty-six ballots had been cast, and then only because Hamilton, hating Jefferson less than he hated Burr, swung the Federalist vote in Jefferson's favor.

President at fifty-seven, Jefferson was the first Chief Executive inaugurated in Washington; he was sworn in, ironically, by the arch-Federalist, Chief Justice John Marshall, who had been appointed by Adams in the closing weeks of his administration.

Jefferson, conscious that he and Burr had forged the nation's first viable opposition party, held out the olive branch to old enemies. In a noble Inaugural Address, Jefferson urged conciliation and an end to sectionalism, and tried to set at rest the fear that he planned a new revolution. "We are all republicans," he said, "we are all federalists." Hailing "a rising nation, spread over a wise and fruitful land . . . advancing rapidly to destinies beyond the reach of mortal eye," Jefferson asked an end to political bitterness. "Every difference of opinion," he said, "is not a difference of principle. We have called by different names brethren of the same principle." It was a candid appeal for practical consensus toward shared ends. Jefferson promised "a wise and frugal government, which shall restrain men from injuring one another, [but] which shall leave them otherwise free to regulate their own pursuits." Then Jefferson—the architect of the Kentucky Resolutions, which gave the Union one of its first major hints of nullification—turned to those who had threatened secession in the North. "If there be any among us who would wish to dissolve this Union or to change its republican form, let them stand undisturbed as monuments of the safety with which error of opinion may be tolerated where reason is left free to combat it."

His oath sworn, President Jefferson moved to strike the Federalists down. The Federalist excise tax and Judiciary Act were repealed, several of Adams' midnight judgeship appointments were declared null and void, and victims of the Alien and Sedition Acts were pardoned. By 1803, a political patronage balance had been restored.

Jefferson's first major foreign crisis began in 1801. European commercial powers—and the United States—had long paid Africa's Barbary Coast pirates annual fees to protect their vessels from raids. When the Pasha of Tripoli demanded that America increase its payments, the United States refused, and the Pasha declared war. Jefferson ordered the fleet to the Mediterranean. In 1804, Tripolitans took the American warship *Philadelphia*, which had run aground, and United States frigates bombarded Tripoli. His purpose, Jefferson said, was to bludgeon "the Barbarians of Tripoli to the desire of peace on proper terms by the sufferings of war."

The Philadelphia, *captured and manned by Tripolitans in the war with the Barbary pirates, was destroyed in a fire (below) set by American raiders.*

Later, William Eaton, the American consul at Tunis, marched with a small force from Libya to the Tripolitan town of Derna and seized it. A treaty favorable to the United States was signed in 1805.

Easily the most important event in Jefferson's first term was his purchase of the Louisiana Territory, which doubled the size of the United States. By the Treaty of San Ildefonso in 1800, Spain had ceded to France its rights to the port of New Orleans and, by extension, to the Mississippi and the vast province of Louisiana. Realizing that free navigation of the Mississippi and the use of New Orleans for storage were crucial to the commerce of the nation, and fearful of new French territorial designs in the West, Jefferson moved to purchase New Orleans in 1803. Given two million dollars by Congress to use for that purpose, he dispatched James Monroe to Paris to join Robert Livingston, who was already negotiating with Napoleon.

Livingston was delighted to learn that Napoleon was willing to offer more than just New Orleans. "They ask of me only one town in Louisiana," the dictator declared, "but I already consider the colony as entirely lost." By the time Monroe arrived, France had ceded to the United States the vast continental slice of land from the Mississippi to the Rockies for sixteen million dollars. Aware that his ministers had far exceeded their congressional instructions and

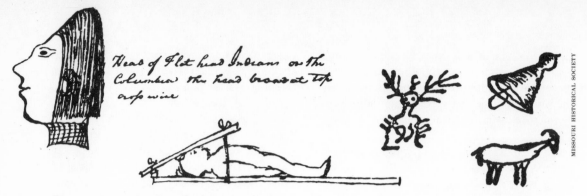

These sketches, taken from the journal of Lewis and Clark, show, from left to right, a flat-headed Chinook; the method used to shape the skulls of infants; a rock painting; an Indian hat; and a bighorn sheep.

constitutional authority, Jefferson decided nevertheless to confront a special session of Congress with the accomplished fact. The Senate and House authorized the purchase, and Jefferson signed the treaty with France on October 20, 1803.

Jefferson's first presidential term was also distinguished by his commissioning of the Lewis and Clark expedition to map the Missouri River and to increase American knowledge of the Western lands. The expedition, begun in May, 1804, concluded when Meriwether Lewis reported to the President on January 10, 1807.

Jefferson, meanwhile, had projected a presidential image wholly new to official Washington. While he served French food—to the chagrin of chauvinists—he also abolished the levee, a quasi-monarchical, ritualistic reception favored by both Presidents Washington and Adams, and maintained in the White House the informality of Monticello. Anthony Merry, Britain's minister, spoke in 1804 of Jefferson's "yarn stockings and slippers down at the heels," describing his general appearance as "very much like that of a tall, large-boned farmer. . . ."

Without question, the diffident patrician had become the hero of America's common man. Jefferson's achievement in gaining this stature was, Dumas Malone has written, "due in considerable part to his identification of himself with causes for which time was fighting. . . . His unchallenged leadership was due, not to self-assertiveness and imperiousness of will, but to the fact that circumstance had made him a symbolic figure, and that to an acute intelligence and

unceasing industry he joined a dauntless and contagious faith."

With a record highlighted by the Louisiana Purchase, the victory over the Barbary pirates, and the repeal of the hated Federalist excise tax, Jefferson sought and decisively won re-election as President in 1804. Burr, who killed Alexander Hamilton in a duel in July, had already been replaced as Jefferson's running mate by New York's governor, George Clinton. The Democratic-Republicans took the South, Pennsylvania, New York, and even conservative Massachusetts, for a total of 162 electoral votes against 14 for Federalists Charles Pinckney and Rufus King. Jefferson could not know then that his second term would end in as much public rancor as his first had ended in exultation.

In 1806 the United States was confronted with naval harassment by both London and Paris, who, blockading each other's ports, seized American ships and impressed American seamen. Jefferson responded with less belligerence than he had shown toward Tripoli: he overtly rejected war with either European power. Though angered in 1807 by Britain's attack on the United States frigate *Chesapeake* and the capture of its crew on the grounds that four of the sailors were British deserters, Jefferson still refused to tarnish his administration with war. His solution was an embargo, terminating all foreign commerce by the United States.

The embargo not only failed to reverse British and French naval policy, but called down the wrath of the nation on Jefferson's head. "A whole people," thundered Josiah Quincy, "is laboring under a most grievous oppression. All the business of the nation is deranged. . . . All its industry stagnant."

"The embargo," writes historian Leonard Levy, "begun as a means of coercing and starving England and France into respect for American rights, rapidly became an instrument of coercion against American citizens. To avoid foreign war, Jefferson made domestic war." The regular army, which Jefferson had opposed, was increased, and the United States Navy and militia were ordered to enforce the embargo. "Congress," the President insisted, "must legalize all *means* which may be necessary to obtain its *end*."

A federal judge in Charleston, himself appointed by Jefferson, attacked the Embargo Act as "an unsanctioned encroachment upon individual liberty." Senator Samuel White of Delaware charged that it put "the whole country under military law," and permitted unwarranted search, seizure, and arrest on the merest suspicion of intent to export. "To this day," Levy concludes, the embargo "remains the most repressive and unconstitutional legislation ever enacted by Congress in time of peace."

By February 21, 1809, Jefferson had asked Congress to lift the embargo against all but French and British shipping, and to lift it entirely by June 1, 1809. It was left to Madison, historian Stuart Gerry Brown notes, "to develop a better policy if he could, or else go to war."

Jefferson's second term was marred by still another major departure from civil liberties. Former Vice President Aaron Burr, who had tried unsuccessfully to lead a revolt of Western states (possibly intending to unite them with Mexico, with himself as emperor of a new kingdom), was tried for treason and acquitted by a federal court under Chief Justice John Marshall. Before the verdict was in, Jefferson made it clear that he thought Burr should be found guilty. It was a grave departure from ideology for the author of *A Summary View* and the Declaration of Independence, and for the man who had successfully urged the adoption of the Bill of Rights, guaranteeing fair trial by jury.

His less-than-splendid second term notwithstanding, many urged Jefferson to seek a third. He declined, however. For Jefferson, the Presidency had been "a splendid misery," bringing "nothing but unceasing drudgery and daily loss of friends."

In retirement at sixty-six, Jefferson became "Old Sachem," the Sage of Monticello. "I resume with delight," he said, "the character and pursuits for which nature designed me. I talk of ploughs and harrows," he wrote in 1810, "of seeding and harvesting, with my neighbors, and of politics, too, if they choose . . . and feel, at length, the blessing of being free to say and do what I please." Old correspondence was renewed. "I have given up newspapers in exchange for Tacitus and Thucydides," he wrote to John Adams in 1812 after their eleven-year silence.

Up at dawn, Jefferson wrote and read until breakfast. He rode six or eight miles on horseback each day, overseeing his lands and farms. He supervised his gristmill, nail factory, and furniture shop; built a dumb-waiter and weather vanes; and delighted in spoiling his beloved great-grandchildren. He kept a full house of family and friends; at times, there were as many as seventy overnight guests. Even in near-bankruptcy—in 1826 his friends throughout the nation raised nearly sixteen thousand dollars to bail him out of debt—he kept Monticello as a haven.

He found time to advise Presidents Madison and Monroe when they asked. But his primary interest in retirement was the founding of the University of Virginia. He

MONTICELLO

A public lottery was initiated in 1826 to bail the ex-President out of debt, but the idea was abandoned when his friends raised some $16,000 themselves.

was involved in the selection of its professors, its library books, its curriculum. He designed its buildings and directly supervised its construction. And he presented at the founding of this first nonsectarian American university a classic definition of academic freedom: "This institution," he said, "will be based on the illimitable freedom of the human mind. For here we are not afraid to follow truth wherever it may lead, nor to tolerate any error so long as reason is left free to combat it."

In retirement, too, Jefferson refined and enlarged his philosophy of freedom. He refused to look back to past authority. "Some men," he wrote, "look at constitutions with sanctimonious reverence, and deem them like the ark of the covenant, too sacred to be touched. . . . Laws and institutions must go hand in hand with the progress of the human mind."

Jefferson retained a vibrant and undiminished faith in democracy. "The only orthodox object . . . of government," he wrote in 1812, "is to secure the greatest degree of happiness possible to the general mass. . . ." Where else, he reasoned, will we "find the origin of *just* powers, if not in the majority of the society?" But although he insisted that the will of the majority prevail, he was equally insistent that the rights of minorities be protected.

Jefferson also retained his faith in the exemplary mission of America. In the Revolution, he maintained, we were not "acting for ourselves alone, but for the whole human race. The event of our experiment is to show whether man can be trusted with self-government."

In his final years, Jefferson held to conservative concepts of federal and state power. Despite his own unorthodox acts as Chief Executive, he insisted that he was opposed to "a very energetic government" as "always oppressive." The states, he maintained, were "the wisest conservative power ever contrived by man."

Jefferson opposed a strong Supreme Court —especially under Federalist control—reviewing the constitutionality of acts passed by an elected Congress and signed by an elected President. "The great object of my fear," he wrote in 1821, "is the Federal Judiciary." He cited the Court's potential reign as an oligarchy, insisting that the Constitution had "erected no such single tribunal," independent of "the will of the nation."

Forced by events to modify soaring theory in searing practice, Jefferson left behind him a rich but paradoxical heritage. Conservatives have admired his opposition to "energetic government," his defense of states' rights, his opposition to the Supreme Court, his frugality with public funds, and his patrician good sense. Liberals have applauded his vigorous use of executive power, his defense of minorities, his commitment to civil liberties, and his defiance of precedent.

It would be facile even to suggest that Jefferson was, or remains, all things to all men. It would be more accurate to say that he has emerged as America's foremost prophet and spokesman of liberty.

For himself, Jefferson remained confident that history would corroborate that men had indeed been created equal and would continue to prefer the "boisterous sea of liberty" to "the calm of despotism." And when all is said, the Jeffersonian tradition, as Boorstin has written, does remain "our principal check on the demands of irresponsible power."

On July 4, 1826, the fiftieth anniversary of the Declaration of Independence, the third President of the United States died, a few hours before his old friend, John Adams. He had fought to stay alive for that day, awaking on the third of July in delirium to mutter instructions that the Virginia Committee of Safety must be warned of the British approach. Ten days before his death, Long Tom wrote one of his last and strongest dicta of liberty. Urging that America remain to the world "the signal of arousing men to burst [their] chains," he said: "The mass of mankind has not been born with saddles on their backs, nor a favored few, booted and spurred, ready to ride them legitimately, by the Grace of God."

—WILSON SULLIVAN

Th Jefferson

A PICTURE PORTFOLIO

This victory flag celebrated Jefferson's assumption of the Presidency after the election of 1800.

"HE SOON SEIZED UPON MY HEART"

"Youth is not rich in time; it may be poor," wrote the poet Edward Young; "Part with it as with money, sparing. . . ." These lines, copied out by Thomas Jefferson in his student days, could stand as the young man's credo, and as an explanation for his rapid rise in colonial politics. He wasted little time, studied diligently, and quickly made his mark. He was practicing law at twenty-three. One year later he became a member of the colonial legislature, and was soon part of the anti-British faction that led the House of Burgesses in its most rebellious acts. His address to George III, *A Summary View of the Rights of British America*, made him a world figure at thirty-one. Draftsman of the Declaration of Independence, and then governor of Virginia, he was chosen to succeed the legendary Franklin as minister to France in 1785. "He was," said John Adams of Jefferson, "so prompt, frank, explicit and decisive upon committees and in conversation . . . that he soon seized upon my heart."

A Swiss painter, Pierre Eugene Du Smitière, made the above portrait of Jefferson in 1775. That same year, the thirty-three-year-old Virginian attended the Continental Congress at Philadelphia and wrote the Declaration of Independence in a room in a bricklayer's house.

The Raleigh Tavern in Williamsburg, above, was a meeting place for the Virginia Revolutionaries. At left is the Governor's Palace, where Jefferson, then a student at William and Mary, often dined with Governor Francis Fauquier. When Jefferson became governor of Virginia during the Revolution, he lived at the Palace.

VIRGINIA PATRIOTS

BOARD OF REGENTS, GUNSTON HALL

SHELBURNE MUSEUM

GEORGE MASON

George Mason's most important achievements were his work on the Virginia constitution and his authorship in 1776 of the Declaration of Rights, which heavily influenced both the Declaration of Independence and the Constitution's Bill of Rights. In the ten preceding years, Mason, a prosperous planter, had played a major role in influencing Virginians in favor of the Revolutionary movement. He eschewed public office, and regarded committees as "overcharged with useless members," but worked for the non-importation of British products, wrote a statement of the colonial position against the Crown (the Fairfax Resolutions), and served on the Committee of Safety, which took power in Virginia in 1775. In the years after the Declaration of Independence, Mason supported acquisition of the Northwest Territory, and worked closely with Wythe, Henry, and Jefferson in preparing new legislation. One of the most active delegates at the Constitutional Convention, he refused to sign the final document because it lacked a bill of rights and because it tolerated slavery, which he considered, "diabolical in itself and disgraceful to mankind." Mason, who died on October 7, 1792, is considered one of the most enlightened and far-sighted of early American statesmen.

PATRICK HENRY

A failure as a planter and store owner, Patrick Henry went on to attain prominence as a lawyer and to become to Virginia in the 1760's what Samuel Adams was to Massachusetts: a leading advocate of separation from England. As a member of the House of Burgesses, Henry vehemently attacked the Stamp Act and the Townshend Acts, and when Governor Dunmore dissolved the House in 1774, he called for a Continental Congress, which he attended as a Virginia delegate. Henry delivered his famous rallying cry, "Give me liberty, or give me death," at a meeting in Richmond in 1775. He attended the Second Continental Congress, and returned to Virginia to help prepare the militia for war. The next year he participated in the drafting of a new state constitution, and continued to press for national independence. Serving five terms as Virginia's governor, he became increasingly conservative. He opposed the federal Constitution on the grounds that it threatened state sovereignty, but when the document was ratified, urged the adoption of the Bill of Rights. A confirmed Federalist in his later years, he feuded with Jefferson, who opposed Washington's policies. Elected to the Virginia House of Delegates in 1799, when he was sixty-three years old, Henry died before taking office.

GEORGE WYTHE

George Wythe was one of the great legal minds of early America. As a judge and as a teacher, he helped formulate American jurisprudence. Admitted to the Virginia bar at the age of twenty, in 1746, Wythe soon began a long career in the Virginia legislature. He helped draft resolutions deploring British tax measures, became a signer of the Declaration of Independence, and was among those who revised Virginia's laws. In 1779 Wythe became professor of law and police at the College of William and Mary, where he lectured on Blackstone and on the differences between English and Virginian law. He was a chancellor of the Virginia high court by 1778, and four years later, in *Commonwealth v. Caton*, he stated clearly the essence of the doctrine of judicial review: "I . . . will say to [the legislature], 'here is the limit of your authority; and hither shall you go but no further.'" A classical scholar of wide repute, Wythe advocated republicanism as opposed to unchecked democracy, echoing Jefferson and Madison. At the Virginia Convention of 1788, he spoke in favor of ratification of the Constitution. Always admired for his incorruptible honesty and disinterestedness, both on the bench and at the bar, he died at eighty, in 1806; in his will, he granted freedom to his slaves.

RICHARD HENRY LEE

A member of an aristocratic Virginia family, Richard Henry Lee joined the House of Burgesses in 1758, and revealed his progressive thinking by advocating that the growth of slavery be checked. He denounced the Stamp Act and other British taxes, and in 1766 formed the Westmoreland Association, the first organization created to boycott British imports. In 1768 he began to urge the establishment of committees of correspondence to keep the colonies apprised of each other's resistance efforts. At the Continental Congress in 1774, Lee was an active member of several important committees; two years later, it was he who made the motion for independence. After helping to form the new government of Virginia, he returned to Philadelphia and proposed measures that would strengthen the union of the states. In subsequent years he became, like Patrick Henry, surprisingly conservative. Re-elected to Congress in 1784, he opposed the Constitution in his "Letters of the Federalist Farmer," because he feared that it would lead to despotism. Serving as a United States senator from 1789 to 1792, he was a supporter of the Bill of Rights, the passage of which eased many of the reservations he had had about the Constitution. Lee died at the age of sixty-two in 1794.

This print, on a cotton kerchief, depicts the adoption of the Declaration of Independence.

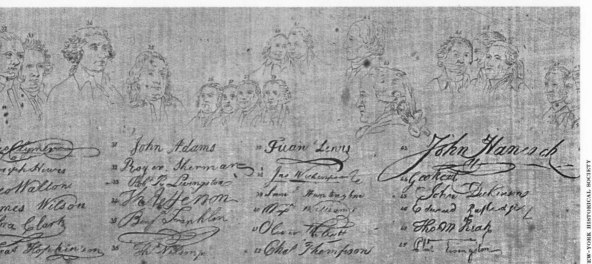

Shown standing in front of the table are Adams, Sherman, Livingston, Jefferson, and Franklin.

Jefferson, a widower, fell in love with the beautiful Maria Cosway, above, during his second summer in France. But she was already married, and their affair was platonic and brief.

"It was wise," Jefferson wrote of France in tumult, "to have 2 passports"—one from the King, one from the elected representatives. The passport below bears the signature of Louis XVI.

A "SAVAGE" ABROAD

Behold me at length on the vaunted scene of Europe!" wrote the new United States minister to France, Thomas Jefferson, to a friend in 1785. "You are, perhaps, curious to know how this new scene has struck a savage of the mountains of America. Not advantageously, I assure you. I find the general fate of humanity here most deplorable." He was shocked by the contrasts in French society. "The truth of Voltaire's observation offers itself perpetually, that every man here must be either the hammer or the anvil," he said. And the quality of the foremost hammers—the royalty—did not impress him. "There is not a crowned head in Europe," he wrote to George Washington in 1788, "whose talents or merits would entitle him to be elected a vestryman by . . . any parish in America." Jefferson remained officially aloof from the revolutionary movement in France, but he sympathized with it and participated as an adviser, particularly in the formation of France's new political institutions. Having toured the provinces, he counseled Lafayette: "Ferret people out of their hovels, as I have done, look into their kettles . . . loll on their beds. . . . You shall [then] be able to apply your knowledge to the softening of their beds, or the throwing a morsel of meat into their kettle of vegetables." Meanwhile, as a diplomat, Jefferson worked out a commercial treaty with Prussia and a consular agreement with France, traveled widely, observed and listened, and sent home a great variety of information on Europe. His stay abroad was both enjoyable and stimulating, and after his return to the United States, the Virginian looked upon France as his second home.

Louis XVI of France, left, was willing to reform his government, and on July 11, 1789, Jefferson wrote that peaceful revolution seemed assured. But the King was easily swayed by advisers. Three days after Jefferson wrote his letter, the Bastille was attacked.

"They took all the arms, discharged the prisoners, and such of the garrison as were not killed in the first moment of fury . . . cut off [the heads of the governor and lieutenant governor] and sent them through the city in triumph." So wrote the American minister, describing the fall of the Bastille, below.

A MOMENTOUS PURCHASE

UNDER ☆ MY ☆ ☆ WINGS

Almost from the start of Washington's administration, Jefferson had criticized the Federalists for stretching the Constitution beyond the intentions of the Founding Fathers. But the major achievement of his own first term as President, the Louisiana Purchase, set a loose-constructionist precedent of profound importance. Jefferson believed that France, which had been given title to Spanish lands beyond the Mississippi, was a threat to American commerce on the river, and he feared that the United States might have to fight a major war to assert its rights of navigation; he was also afraid that European wars might spread to North America if the French retained the Louisiana region. The President saw the future of the United States in continental terms; two years before the purchase was made he had begun to plan an expedition to explore the Northwest to the Pacific. When it seemed that Napoleon might be willing to sell Florida and some of the land on the lower Mississippi, Jefferson sent American diplomats to France to open negotiations, even though the Constitution did not mention a federal right to buy new territory. But when the United States was suddenly offered 828,000 square miles of land, extending westward to the Rockies, the President agonized over the constitutional question. He considered asking for an amendment to legalize the act, and finally supported the purchase, hoping, he said, "that the good sense of our country will correct the evil of loose construction when it shall produce its ill effects."

☆EVERY☆ ☆THING☆ PROSPERS

New Orleans (above) was a prosperous city in 1803, the year it became American. The strategic location of this port, controlling all the ocean-bound trade of the Mississippi, was one reason for the Louisiana Purchase.

JEFFERSON'S APPOINTEES

ROBERT R. LIVINGSTON

Robert R. Livingston's role in the negotiation of the Louisiana Purchase in 1803 capped a notable public career. He had served on a wide range of committees during four terms in the Continental Congress, and he had helped draft the Declaration of Independence, although he did not sign it because the New York convention had not so authorized him. Livingston then organized the new nation's department of foreign affairs and, as its first foreign secretary, oversaw the signing of the Treaty of Paris. He was a key figure in the formation of New York's state government, helping to draw up its constitution. From 1777 to 1801 he was New York State chancellor, in which capacity he administered the presidential oath to George Washington in 1789. Livingston split with the Federalists because he felt that he had not received his just share of patronage and became Jefferson's minister to France in 1801. When Napoleon offered to sell all of Louisiana to the United States, Livingston, along with James Monroe, boldly exceeded his authority and accepted. He had backed Robert Fulton's development of the steamship *Clermont*, and when he retired in 1804 Livingston continued to exercise the monopoly on steam navigation he had obtained from the state of New York in 1798. He died in 1813 at the age of sixty-six.

ALBERT GALLATIN

Swiss-born Albert Gallatin came to America in 1780 when he was nineteen; by 1790 he was a member of the Pennsylvania legislature, evincing a Jeffersonian liberalism and an interest in public finance. Elected to the United States Senate in 1794, he demanded that the Secretary of the Treasury issue reports on past expenses, and was unseated by Federalists who maintained that he had not been a citizen long enough to serve in the Senate. A congressman from 1795 to 1801, Gallatin helped create a standing finance committee and continued to urge financial reforms. As Secretary of the Treasury under Jefferson and Madison, he favored light taxes and little spending; but although he reduced the national debt, the prewar embargoes and the War of 1812 ruined his attempts to bring about lasting fiscal stability. He served on the peace delegation to Ghent, negotiated commercial treaties with Britain, and became minister to France and then to England. Returning to America, he served from 1831 until 1839 as president of the National Bank. Gallatin was also the first president of the University of the City of New York, the founder of the American Ethnological Society, and the president of the New-York Historical Society. In the last years of his life, he conducted valuable studies of Indian tribes. He died in 1849.

MERIWETHER LEWIS

At twenty-nine, Meriwether Lewis was pre-eminently qualified for the task assigned him in 1803 by Thomas Jefferson: to lead an overland expedition to the Pacific. Lewis, raised in Virginia and Georgia, was an expert hunter and amateur naturalist. Six years in various military outposts had tested his leadership and familiarized him with Indian affairs. Lewis had become Jefferson's private secretary in 1801, and they frequently discussed Jefferson's long-held dream of Northwest exploration. In the spring of 1804, forty-eight men under Lewis and William Clark began their trek to the headwaters of the Missouri River and beyond. They wintered in North Dakota and by August of 1805 approached the Continental Divide. They descended the Clearwater and Columbia rivers, reaching the Pacific Ocean in November. On the return trip, Lewis took a different route than Clark and encountered hostile Indians. Later he was accidentally wounded by one of his own men; but the parties rejoined and arrived in St. Louis in September of 1806 to the surprise and joy of a country that had presumed them lost. Lewis had justified Jefferson's faith in him by making voluminous notes which were of great value to scientists, explorers, and students. He became governor of Louisiana, a post he held until his death in 1809.

WILLIAM CLARK

William Clark was happily surprised when Meriwether Lewis asked him to help lead an expedition to the Northwest in 1803. The younger brother of George Rogers Clark, he had served in the Army from 1792 to 1796, and had participated in several fierce battles with the Indians, including the one at Fallen Timbers in Ohio in 1794, during which he had met Lewis for the first time. After retiring from the Army, Clark had traveled widely in the West, and Lewis knew that his thorough knowledge of Indian affairs and his experiences as a frontiersman made him an ideal choice for co-leader of the exploration party. Clark's bent for map making and his skill at drawing birds and animals also contributed heavily to the mission's success. After the expedition's return in 1806, Clark became superintendent of Indian affairs for the Louisiana (later Missouri) Territory; in 1813, he became governor of the region. During the War of 1812, Clark was instrumental in defending the West from British-incited Indian attacks. Postwar treaties were periodically broken by rebellious tribes, but Clark often took the side of the Indians against the federal government, and as a result won their esteem and kept uprisings to a minimum. Clark remained active in Western affairs until his death at the age of sixty-eight on September 1, 1838.

In the war with the Barbary States, the former American consul at Tunis, William Eaton, carried out an incredible unauthorized military mission against Tripoli. He marched a patchwork army five hundred miles across the desert (above) from Alexandria to Derna, which he captured, helping to bring about a peace treaty.

A TROUBLED TERM

Foreign affairs made Jefferson's second term a rocky one. The Napoleonic Wars resulted in restrictions on American shipping by the belligerents, impressment of American sailors, and the British attack on the frigate *Chesapeake*. Jefferson responded with the Nonimportation and Embargo acts, but these were not effective and were bitterly resented by many Americans. There were some successes, however: a treaty was signed with the Barbary pirates; Spain was induced to cease harassing the Southern and Western frontiers; and Congress made it illegal to import slaves. But by 1809 Jefferson was glad to be leaving office. "Never did a prisoner, released from his chains, feel such relief as I shall on shaking off the shackles of power," he wrote on March 2. "Nature intended me," the President added wistfully, "for the tranquil pursuits of science. . . ."

In 1805 Jefferson found himself in the midst of the war between England and France. The above cartoon, symbolic of the war's effect on American trade, depicts King George and Napoleon robbing the President.

On June 22, 1807, the American frigate Chesapeake sailed out of Hampton Roads, Virginia, bound for the Mediterranean, with four British sailors in her crew. She was intercepted by the British Leopard, and when she refused permission for a search, the Leopard fired a crippling broadside (left) and seized the four deserters. American anger at the incident led to the embargo.

123

JUDICIAL GIANT

John Marshall had "one original . . . almost supernatural faculty," said a contemporary, William Wirt: he could grasp an argument in a law court by "a single glance of his mind." This amazing capacity for concentration and insight was obvious to others even in Marshall's youth: he needed only about a month's formal study and a few years of practice to become one of Virginia's leading lawyers. And although he had never held a judicial post prior to his appointment to the Supreme Court, he became a superb Chief Justice.

Born near Germantown, Virginia, in 1755, Marshall served in the Revolution as an officer, was elected a state assemblyman, and was Virginia's most prominent Federalist by the time he was forty. Although he turned down several important national posts because he preferred to practice law, he did agree to accept an assignment to France in 1797, a mission that resulted in the XYZ Affair. He was elected to Congress in 1799, and in May, 1800, President John Adams convinced Marshall to become Secretary of State; the following year, Adams made him, concurrently, Chief Justice. It was Marshall, therefore, who swore in his distant cousin and political enemy, Thomas Jefferson, as the nation's third President.

Out of the Jefferson-Marshall antagonism came one of the Supreme Court's most momentous precedents: that the Court could declare an act of Congress unconstitutional. John Adams had spent his final night in the White House making last-gasp appointments designed to preserve Federalist power in the government. Among them were a number of justices of the peace for the District of Columbia. In the rush, some of the commissions were never delivered, and Jefferson decided to hold on to them. One of the men waiting for his commission was William Marbury; he asked the Supreme Court to demand that Secretary of State Madison deliver the commissions, being aware that the Court had been empowered to do so by the Judiciary Act of 1789. Marshall was sympathetic, but he knew that the Court was at a crossroads in terms of prestige, and that if it did issue the order, Jefferson and Madison would ignore it. He did not want to rule against Marbury, so he delivered his precedent-setting opinion, *Marbury v. Madison*, in which he scathingly criticized Madison and Jefferson for not giving Marbury his commission, but declared that the section of law that empowered the Court to issue the order was unconstitutional. Jefferson called Marshall's careful logic "twistifications," but Marshall had made the first assertion of what was to be the greatest power of the Supreme Court.

Marshall served as Chief Justice for more than thirty-four years. It was very much his Court; of 1,106 decisions handed down, he dissented on only 9. He established protections for private property; he expanded the powers of the federal government and restricted those of the states; most important, although he never again found it necessary to declare a law unconstitutional, he made the Court the nation's final arbiter on the acceptability of laws.

John Marshall, portrayed by Rembrandt Peale

When one pen on the polygraph above was moved, the other moved in the same way. Jefferson adapted the machine so that he could make copies of his letters as he wrote them.

Below is a page from one product of Jefferson's study of American Indian languages—a comparative vocabulary. In the left-hand column the languages are identified, followed by the different words for "fog," "rain," and "snow."

English	fog	rain	snow
French	brouillard	pluie	neige
Delaware	áòuàn	suuklan	uúna
Miami		su-ke-laan	quun
Monsi		su-ke-laan	quun
Chippewa		ke-me-wàn	ac-quun
Killisteneaux	pakishikow	kimiwoin	counak
Algonquin	awinni	ke mi woini	so quu po
Tawa		ki-mi-wàn	ac-quun
Shawanee		ki-mĕ-waini kimmawane	quun-ĕ looke
Nanticoke	hous̃e,wen	uiniqw su-ke-ran	quá-no quun
Mohiccon		sohangan so-ke-gan	washaná wa-scha-ni
Onguackog		suhehun	soáchpo
Oneida	Liahwanianah	yoconnoal	onaieghta
Cayuga			
Onondaga	ginquara tiawenohku	na-jelahtaronti	ogésa
Miami	uoonuah	petilénivé petilomnah	monétwa monatush
Cherokee		oc ciais cuh kounshan	ainheche aim

"ALWAYS DOING"

John F. Kennedy once described a group of Nobel Prize winners, dining in the Executive Mansion, as "the most extraordinary collection of talent . . . that has ever been gathered together at the White House—with the possible exception of when Thomas Jefferson dined alone." Merely dipping at random into Jefferson's achievements in the arts and sciences reveals the variety of his talents. He developed a distinctively American style of architecture by combining Roman models with inexpensive American materials. His experiments with rice growing (for which he once smuggled seeds out of Italy) made the United States a major rice producer, and his ideas on education and architecture were embodied in the University of Virginia. The urge to learn and to educate others led him in many directions. From 1797 to 1815, he served as president of the American Philosophical Society, a scientific organization. He collected the bones of prehistoric animals, Indian vocabularies, paintings and sculpture, and great books (his library formed the basis of the new Library of Congress after the first had been burned by the British in 1814). And his writings cover a vast range of subjects, including morals, botany, legislative procedure, comparative literature, philosophy, and marriage. As Jefferson himself once wrote, "Determine never to be idle. . . . It is wonderful how much may be done if we are always doing."

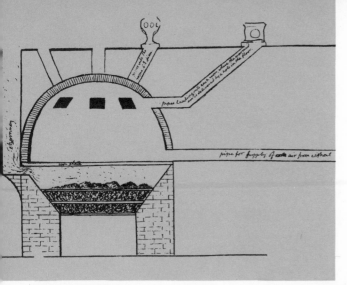

The central-heating plant, left, was another of Jefferson's inventions. The upward shafts are a chimney and heat pipes; the horizontal one carried air to the fire.

Jefferson's design for the rotunda at the University of Virginia, below, was derived from Palladio's drawing of the Roman Pantheon. However, the rotunda design was considerably less massive than that of its classical model, with taller pillars, a simpler portico, and a more graceful unity.

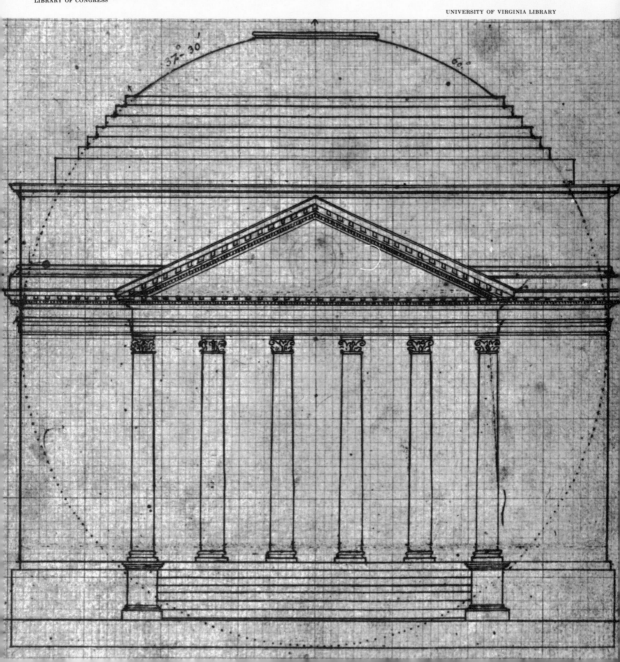

Monticello ("little mountain") was begun in 1769 and was livable, though uncompleted, when Jefferson left for France. His travels gave him new ideas for the mansion, and work on it was renewed while he was Secretary of State. Not until his Presidency was over did the thirty-two-room house (below) assume its final form.

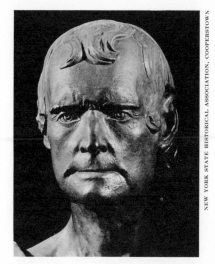

*John H. I. Browere made the life mask
of Jefferson, above, in October, 1825.*

MONTICELLO

Jefferson, declared the
Marquis de Chastellux after visiting Monticello in 1782, "is the first American who
has consulted the Fine Arts to know how he
should shelter himself from the weather."
Seven years later, Jefferson began a major
remodeling of his home, finally finishing it in
1808. In addition to the classical design, Jefferson was responsible for such ingenious de-
vices as clocks that told the day as well as
the hour, folding ladders, a dumb-waiter
(hidden in a fireplace) on which wine could
be elevated from the cellar, swivel chairs,
and hanging beds. In 1809 he retired to
Monticello, where, until he died in 1826, he
played the genial and generous host, while
falling ever further into debt. Captain Edmund Bacon, his overseer, felt that the
Sage's "gangs" of guests took advantage of
him. They came year round, but were most
numerous in summer. Bacon remarked that
the twenty-six spare horse stalls at Monticello were frequently not sufficient for the
visitors' mounts. "I have often sent a wagon-
load of hay up to the stable," the overseer
said, "and the next morning there would not
be enough left to make a bird's nest."

FACTS IN SUMMARY: THOMAS JEFFERSON

CHRONOLOGY

UNITED STATES		JEFFERSON
	1743	Born April 13
	1762	Graduates from College of William and Mary
Townshend Acts	1767	Admitted to the bar
	1768	Elected to Virginia House of Burgesses
Boston Massacre	1770	Appointed Albemarle County lieutenant
	1772	Marries Martha Skelton
Boston Tea Party	1773	Appointed Albemarle County surveyor
First Continental Congress	1774	Writes A Summary View of the Rights of British America
Lexington and Concord	1775	Elected alternate delegate to Second Continental Congress
Second Continental Congress		
Declaration of Independence	1776	Drafts Declaration of Independence
		Elected to Virginia House of Delegates
Articles of Confederation adopted	1777	
	1779	Introduces Act for Establishing Religious Freedom
		Elected governor of Virginia
British invade Virginia	1781	Resigns as governor
Siege of Yorktown		
Treaty of Paris	1783	Drafts Virginia constitution
		Elected to Continental Congress
	1785	Named minister to France
Constitutional Convention	1787	
Washington elected President	1789	Appointed Secretary of State
Bill of Rights		
	1791	Leads opposition to Hamilton
Genêt Affair	1793	Resigns Secretaryship
Adams wins Presidency	1796	Elected Vice President
Naval war with France	1798	Drafts Kentucky Resolutions
Alien and Sedition Acts		
Treaty of Morfontaine	1800	Ties with Burr in presidential election
Tripoli declares war against U.S.	1801	Elected President
		Dispatches Navy to Mediterranean
	1802	Repeals excise tax and Judiciary Act of 1801
Ohio admitted as 17th state	1803	Approves Louisiana Purchase
Louisiana Purchase		Commissions Lewis and Clark expedition
Burr-Hamilton duel	1804	Re-elected President
Peace with Tripoli	1805	
Chesapeake-Leopard Affair	1807	Signs Embargo Act
Madison inaugurated	1809	Signs Nonintercourse Act
Washington burned	1814	Sells books to Congress
	1819	Becomes rector of University of Virginia
John Adams dies July 4	1826	Dies July 4

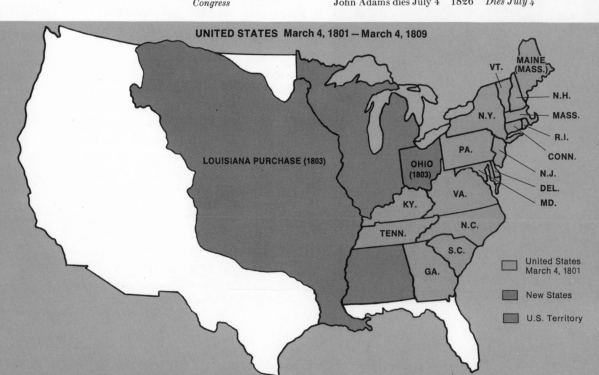

UNITED STATES March 4, 1801 — March 4, 1809

LOUISIANA PURCHASE (1803)

OHIO (1803)

VT. · MAINE (MASS.) · N.H. · N.Y. · MASS. · R.I. · PA. · CONN. · N.J. · DEL. · MD. · VA. · KY. · TENN. · N.C. · S.C. · GA.

☐ United States March 4, 1801
■ New States
■ U.S. Territory

BIOGRAPHICAL FACTS

BIRTH: "Shadwell," Goochland (now Albemarle) County, Virginia, April 13, 1743

ANCESTRY: Welsh

FATHER: Peter Jefferson; b. Chesterfield County, Va., Feb. 29, 1708; d. "Shadwell," Va., Aug. 17, 1757

FATHER'S OCCUPATION: Planter; surveyor

MOTHER: Jane Randolph Jefferson; b. London, England, Feb. 9, 1720; d. "Shadwell," Va., March 31, 1776

BROTHER: Randolph (1755-1815)

SISTERS: Jane (1740-1765); Mary (1741-1760); Martha (1746-1811); Lucy (1752-1784); Anna Scott (1755-?)

WIFE: Martha Wayles Skelton; b. Charles City County, Va., Oct. 19, 1748; d. "Monticello," Va., Sept. 6, 1782

MARRIAGE: Charles City County, Va., Jan. 1, 1772

CHILDREN: Martha (1772-1836); Maria (1778-1804); Lucy Elizabeth (1782-1785); (two daughters and a son died in infancy)

HOME: "Monticello," Charlottesville, Va.

EDUCATION: Private tutoring; attended country school in Albemarle County, Va.; received B.A. from College of William and Mary (1762)

RELIGIOUS AFFILIATION: No denomination

OCCUPATIONS BEFORE PRESIDENCY: Planter; lawyer; writer; philosopher; scientist; architect

PRE-PRESIDENTIAL OFFICES: Member of Virginia House of Burgesses; County Lieutenant; County Surveyor; Deputy Delegate to Second Continental Congress; Member of Virginia House of Delegates; Governor of Virginia; Commissioner to France; Minister to France; Secretary of State; Vice President

POLITICAL PARTY: Democratic-Republican

AGE AT INAUGURATION: 57

OCCUPATIONS AFTER PRESIDENCY: Planter; writer; educator

DEATH: "Monticello," Charlottesville, Va., July 4, 1826

PLACE OF BURIAL: "Monticello," Charlottesville, Va.

ELECTION OF 1800

(Each elector voted for two men. A tie between Jefferson and Burr resulted, and the House of Representatives elected Jefferson President.)

CANDIDATES	ELECTORAL VOTE
Thomas Jefferson Democratic-Republican	73
Aaron Burr Democratic-Republican	73
John Adams Federalist	65
Charles C. Pinckney Federalist	64
John Jay Federalist	1

FIRST ADMINISTRATION

INAUGURATION: March 4, 1801; Senate Chamber, Washington, D.C.

VICE PRESIDENT: Aaron Burr

SECRETARY OF STATE: James Madison

SECRETARY OF THE TREASURY: Samuel Dexter; Albert Gallatin (from May 14, 1801)

SECRETARY OF WAR: Henry Dearborn

ATTORNEY GENERAL: Levi Lincoln

POSTMASTER GENERAL: Joseph Habersham; Gideon Granger (from Nov. 28, 1801)

SECRETARY OF THE NAVY: Benjamin Stoddert; Robert Smith (from July 27, 1801)

SUPREME COURT APPOINTMENT: William Johnson (1804)

SEVENTH CONGRESS (March 4, 1801-March 4, 1803): Senate: 18 Democratic-Republicans; 14 Federalists House: 69 Democratic-Republicans; 36 Federalists

EIGHTH CONGRESS (March 4, 1803-March 4, 1805): Senate: 25 Democratic-Republicans; 9 Federalists House: 102 Democratic-Republicans; 39 Federalists

STATE ADMITTED: Ohio (1803)

END OF PRESIDENTIAL TERM: March 4, 1805

ELECTION OF 1804

(The Twelfth Amendment, ratified in September, 1804, provided for separate voting for President and Vice President, and precluded a repetition of the Jefferson-Burr tie of 1800.)

CANDIDATES	ELECTORAL VOTE
Thomas Jefferson Democratic-Republican	162
Charles C. Pinckney Federalist	14

SECOND ADMINISTRATION

INAUGURATION: March 4, 1805; Senate Chamber, Washington, D.C.

VICE PRESIDENT: George Clinton

SECRETARY OF STATE: James Madison

SECRETARY OF THE TREASURY: Albert Gallatin

SECRETARY OF WAR: Henry Dearborn

ATTORNEY GENERAL: John Breckinridge: Caesar A. Rodney (from Jan. 20, 1807)

POSTMASTER GENERAL: Gideon Granger

SECRETARY OF THE NAVY: Robert Smith

SUPREME COURT APPOINTMENTS: Brockholst Livingston (1806); Thomas Todd (1807)

NINTH CONGRESS (March 4, 1805-March 4, 1807): Senate: 27 Democratic-Republicans; 7 Federalists House: 116 Democratic-Republicans; 25 Federalists

TENTH CONGRESS (March 4, 1807-March 4, 1809): Senate: 28 Democratic-Republicans; 6 Federalists House: 118 Democratic-Republicans; 24 Federalists

END OF PRESIDENTIAL TERM: March 4, 1809

JAMES MADISON

As Father of the Constitution, congressman, chief organizer of the Democratic-Republican party, Secretary of State, and President, James Madison was, figuratively, a giant in the history of the United States. Physically, however, he was (in the words of Washington Irving) a "withered little apple-John." Brittle and sickly, at five feet six and barely one hundred pounds he was the smallest of the American Presidents. He had bright blue eyes under bushy eyebrows, a pale complexion, scraggly white hair, and lips permanently pinched as though pursed in unending contemplation. A naturally restrained delivery combined with a slight vocal disability made his speeches almost inaudible.

But what James Madison had to say was usually worth hearing. A bookish man, most at ease in his library, he was nonetheless a good conversationalist, knowledgeable of course, but witty, earthy, and satirical, too. He might have preferred a discussion of Greek philosophy with his friend Thomas Jefferson, but he was quite capable of making small talk with his wife's guests and charming them with his ingratiating smile.

Born in his maternal grandmother's home at Port Conway, Virginia, on March 16, 1751, he was, like Washington and Jefferson, a scion of the powerful planter aristocracy. The Madison plantation in the Virginia Piedmont stretched for thousands of acres and touched the wild Appalachian frontier at Montpelier, site of the wooden house where James was raised. His mother taught him to read and write, and his father, a justice of the peace, taught him by example the obligations to community service that the planter class assumed. He had plenty of playmates, almost all of whom were children of his father's slaves. At night he often lay awake in fear, listening to the Indian raiding parties emerging from the mountain forests close by, their spine-chill-

President Madison, by John Vanderlyn

ing war whoops echoing through the valley. Both the companionship of his boyhood days and the trauma of the nights made lasting impressions on James Madison: as an adult he would remain at once bitterly anti-Indian and emphatically antislavery.

At the age of eleven, Madison was sent to the school of Donald Robertson, a Scot who spoke English and other languages with so pronounced a burr that James joked about having to learn "Scottish French." After 1767, however, Madison was educated at home under the tutelage of young Reverend Thomas Martin, Princeton, class of 1764.

Virginia gentry customarily sent their sons either abroad to college or to William and Mary in Williamsburg; to send them to school in another colony was almost tantamount to treason. But in 1769, when he was eighteen, James Madison entered the College of New Jersey at Princeton. His father claimed that the climate of Williamsburg was the primary reason; but while it was true that James was frail and sickly, "climate" may have had a double meaning. William and Mary's administration was doing nothing to stop the violent persecution of Virginia Baptists, and its Episcopalian president was known to favor the establishment of a state church, which the Madisons opposed.

Unlike William and Mary, which catered almost exclusively to Virginians, Princeton attracted students from all the colonies. There Madison began to understand the absurdity of the idea—much too prevalent— that one owed all his patriotic allegiance to his native province. In the same way, Princeton's theological broad-mindedness and avowed tolerance of religious dissent confirmed Madison's conviction that no sect could claim a privileged place in any society.

Madison was a dedicated student, a natural scholar who retained and applied what he learned. At Princeton he studied Locke and Montesquieu and, like Jefferson, could, when the time came, immediately apply their philosophies to the reality of the American situation. John Locke held that every nation is a compact between government and governed: should one party violate the compact, the other is entitled to react in any way deemed necessary to secure his rights. Investigating the machinery of free government, Baron de Montesquieu (Charles Luis de Secondat) concluded that maintenance of freedom depended on a separation of executive, legislative, and judicial powers so that each could check and balance the others.

After receiving his B.A. in 1771, Madison considered becoming a minister, and he remained at Princeton for another year to study Hebrew and ethics. He changed his mind about the ministry, however, and returned home in doubt about his future. His studies and extracurricular interests had weakened his physical condition, and his deteriorated health left him tense, depressed, and uncertain for more than two years.

Then came the Revolution. American independence was to James Madison a great moral and philosophical cause, and it was also a strength-building, restorative tonic. Too weak to carry a musket, he shouldered the burdens of statesmanship.

On January 2, 1775, Madison was present at the meeting of the Orange County Com-

COURTESY OF ALBERT E. LEEDS

The above miniature of Madison was painted sometime between 1780 and 1783 by Charles Wilson Peale.

Montpelier, Madison's home in Virginia, was depicted by the Baroness Hyde de Neuville, wife of the French minister to the United States, in 1818.

mittee of Safety at which his father was elected chairman. Seventeen months later Madison attended the Virginia Convention of 1776, which within a month's time made two crucial decisions: on May 15 it instructed the Virginia delegates to the Continental Congress to declare for independence from Great Britain, and on June 12 it passed the Virginia Declaration of Rights, which established fundamental guarantees of personal liberty and later became the model for the Bill of Rights. The chief draftsman of the Declaration of Rights was George Mason, but Madison prompted a subtle but important change in the wording of one key passage. While Mason had wanted to ensure governmental "toleration" of religious dissent, Madison prevailed on the Convention to have the passage state that "all men are equally entitled to the free exercise of religion, according to the dictates of conscience."

Madison was the youngest delegate to the Continental Congress, which in 1781 established a government of the United States. He was well aware, however, that the Articles of Confederation were imperfect. Because the powers to tax, regulate commerce, and raise armies had been left to the states, the federal government was impotent to enforce legislation until the states decided to supply the means for enforcement.

On May 25, 1787, the Constitutional Convention convened in Philadelphia. Among the fifty-five delegates were some who wanted broad, almost authoritarian power conferred on a central government and others who favored retention of state sovereignty and wanted only to close the loopholes of the Articles of Confederation; most delegates occupied positions somewhere between. The most effective debater, dialectician, and advocate of a strong new constitution was James Madison, who had been instrumental in calling the Convention and who had written extensively about the defects of the Articles of Confederation.

Convention sessions were held behind closed doors, and discussions were not recorded; but Madison kept notes on the principal proceedings. His own speeches were among the most significant, containing as they did such passages as this on the system of checks and balances: "A people deliberating in a temperate moment, and with the experience of other nations before them, on the plan of government most likely to secure their happiness, would first be aware that those charged with the public happiness might betray their trust. An obvious precaution against this danger would be to divide the trust between different bodies of men, who might watch and check each other."

That the President, Congress, and Supreme Court would form the three branches of the government was agreed upon with comparatively little dispute, but the composition of the legislature did not so easily emerge from the debates. The Virginia Plan, which Madison had written, suggested representation proportionate to population; the New Jersey Plan retained the Confederation system of one-state one-vote. Connecticut delegates proposed an acceptable compromise, which incorporated both plans in a two-chambered legislature. But another problem remained: since Congress had decided to apportion the House of Representatives on the basis of total population (as opposed to number of voters), the Southerners claimed that slaves should be counted, while the Northerners (paradoxically) had to take the position that a slave did not belong to the population at all. The compromise, which Madison had suggested as early as 1783, declared five slaves equal to three freemen in congressional apportionment.

Although he was largely responsible for it, the idea that the Constitution of his country contained wording that made a Negro three-fifths of a man must have been repugnant to James Madison, who pleaded for the "eventual extinguishment of slavery in the United States." But he conceived the "federal ratio" because he cared most about forging a strong national government.

The signing of the document on September 17, 1787, was only the first step in effecting it. Each state had to ratify it; and however awesome it seems today, the Constitution was by no means without opponents at its inception. At the Virginia Ratification Convention Madison promised to press for a series of amendments protecting individual freedom. His speeches helped secure the necessary votes. True to his word, he later led the fight for the Bill of Rights.

With Hamilton and John Jay, Madison contributed to a series of articles that during 1787 and 1788 appeared in the New York press over the signature "Publius." Probably the most persuasive of all defenses of the Constitution, the series was published in a single volume called *The Federalist*. Madison's tenth *Federalist* essay attracted the most attention. His theme was the danger that one group might gain domination over the nation. Developing his ideas in a tight, reasonable sequence, he found the antidote to be the tri-branched, two-housed political arrangement made possible by the Constitution. When New York ratified on July 26, 1788, much of the credit belonged to *The Federalist*.

In 1788 Madison was elected to the House of Representatives. During his four terms

there, the Federalist party formed behind Hamilton. It was Madison who organized the followers of Jefferson's opposing philosophy into the Democratic-Republican party. During the stormy administration of John Adams, Madison fought against the Alien and Sedition Acts. To counter their effectiveness, he wrote the Virginia Resolutions, which assumed for states the right to refuse to comply with a law they deemed unconstitutional.

When Jefferson entered the White House in 1801, Madison became his Secretary of State. Although the affairs of state during his eight years in the Cabinet were of lasting significance, they cannot, be honestly credited to Madison, for Jefferson chose to be his own Secretary of State. But if Madison's achievements in the Jefferson administration were negligible, they were at least not political hindrances; and in the election of 1808, with the support of Jefferson, Madison ran for President, defeating Charles Cotesworth Pinckney, the Federalist candidate, by an electoral vote of 122 to 47.

James Madison was, of course, new to the duties of the Presidency, but his wife, Dolley, was used to being the First Lady, since she had acted as Jefferson's hostess. Madison had married Mrs. Dolley Payne Todd, a widow, on September 15, 1794, just three months after he had written a letter to a mutual acquaintance, Aaron Burr, asking him to arrange a meeting. As First Lady, Mrs. Madison began to entertain on a lavish scale, dazzling Washington with the splendid formality of her state dinners and the gay spontaneity of her private parties.

The gaiety of the White House social functions did not, however, reflect the atmosphere of Madison's administration. Like the three Chief Executives before him, the President found himself deeply involved in issues connected with European wars. England's Orders in Council assumed for British ships the right to stop and search neutral, specifically American, vessels suspected of bearing contraband, and Napoleon declared that an American ship that permitted itself to be boarded by the British would be con-

"TO THE GRAVE GO SHAM PROTECTORS OF " FREE TRADE AND SAILORS RIGHTS"—AND ALL THE PEOPLE SAY AMEN !"

The cartoon above shows Madison being dragged down by the unpopular Anglo-American trade restrictions.

sidered fair game for French guns. The one issue that cut deepest into the young nation's pride was the impressment of American sailors: British naval officers dismissed the validity of naturalization papers and, on boarding American ships, pressed into service any sailor who acted suspiciously or spoke or looked like an Englishman. Jefferson's embargo had been no solution, for it evaded confrontation only at the expense of the economy and national pride. Repealed in 1809, three days before Madison's inauguration, it was replaced by the Nonintercourse Act, which reopened trade with all nations except France and England and gave the President authority to restore trade whenever either or both belligerents withdrew its edicts against American shipping. When neither did so, Congress naïvely sought to force their hands by passing, in 1810, Macon's Bill No. 2, which restored trade with the warring powers and gave them until March 3, 1811, to revoke their edicts. Should one of the powers acquiesce, the President of the United States would declare a ninety-day suspension of trade with the other, and if its decrees were not withdrawn in that time, America would revive the Nonintercourse Act against the offending nation. Calculated to play France and England against each other, the bill in reality gave them a year to trade with the United States

and to harass American ships with impunity.

The country was sharply divided in its sympathies. New England Federalists were, as usual, anti-French; the Republicans—especially those of the frontier states—remained anti-English. Ironically, despite the fact that the growing rallying cry for war was "free trade and sailors' rights," shippers in the Northeast were quite unready for war. They blamed Republican incompetence for their troubles more than they did British intervention, and they were making enough profit from the ships that penetrated the blockade to make up for their losses. The Westerners, on the other hand, many of whom had never seen a ship, were most militant. Led by Henry Clay of Kentucky, these "war hawks" talked about national pride, but they thought about national expansion and looked longingly to Canada and West Florida.

The United States wanted Florida, and the Napoleonic Wars provided an excuse to begin taking it. On October 27, 1810, after receiving word that the people of Spanish West Florida (most of whom were American and French) had declared independence, President Madison signed a proclamation declaring West Florida American territory. The area, Madison claimed, had officially been American since the Louisiana Purchase.

Meanwhile, in the Northwest, Governor William Henry Harrison of the Indiana Territory was having trouble with the Indians. Upset that the Indians had the audacity to regard a 1795 boundary agreement as binding, Harrison wrote to Madison that Tecumseh—the Shawnee chief who was inciting many tribes by advocating unity, firmness in regard to land sales, abstinence from alcohol, and other radical measures—was "insolent and his pretensions arrogant." There could be, to Harrison and much of the nation, only one force behind Tecumseh's hostility: Great Britain. At first Madison turned down Harrison's request for permission to assault the Indian Territory because he did not want to divert troops from West Florida, but in 1811 he gave the go-ahead, and on November 7 Harrison engaged the

Shawnee and their allies in the bloody Battle of Tippecanoe.

While America waited for French and English replies to Macon's Bill, the nation prospered from the increased customs receipts resulting from the resumption of trade. Prosperity hung by a thread, however, because the charter of the Bank of the United States was due to expire on March 4, 1811. As Madison's biographer, Irving Brant, points out, the President was a victim of a "lifelong unwillingness to make a public display of political inconsistency." With war a possibility, and with the country's money interests so obviously opposed to war with the probable enemy, Madison needed the Bank and wanted it rechartered; but he would not appear before Congress to make his wants known, for he had once denied the constitutionality of the Bank. When the Senate voted 17 to 17 on recharter, Vice President George Clinton broke the tie with a negative vote. As the Bank went out of existence, a depression began, hitting hard in the frontier states.

In December, 1810, after agreeing to honor American shipping rights (thereby compelling America to declare nonintercourse with England), Napoleon sequestered all American ships in French ports and declared all ports in the French alliance closed to American trade. With impenetrable logic, the Emperor claimed that his actions were designed to compel Britain to revoke its Orders in Council. The effects of Macon's Bill had backfired: now France was in the strong position and throughout the year made only minor concessions to the United States. Britain, meanwhile, claimed that France had not in fact revoked its decrees (which it had not); and American Federalists said that France was the enemy, not England, and that Madison had been tricked by Napoleon (which he had) into an anti-English posture. Nevertheless, the President held firm and demanded that Parliament repeal the Orders in Council. Faced with serious economic problems at home, British Prime Minister Spencer Perceval finally decided to endorse repeal, but was assassinated

before he could act. It was not until June 16, 1812, that England withdrew the orders.

A day later the United States declared war. On June 1, President Madison had appeared in Congress to list "the spectacle of injuries and indignities which have been heaped on our country. . . ." Deploring the fact that "our moderation and conciliation have had no other effect than to encourage perseverance and to enlarge pretentions," he placed the decision of "opposing force . . . in defense of national rights" into the hands of Congress. So war was declared after the principal acknowledged reason for war had been removed. In those days of slow communications, word of the repeal of the Orders in Council did not arrive until later.

National division, reflected in the congressional war vote—79 to 49 in the House, 19 to 13 in the Senate—prevailed throughout the War of 1812. Although it had wanted war, Congress was sluggish about voting funds to increase the size of the Army and Navy; and just as the frontier states united to wage war, the New England states united in refusing to have anything to do with it. In the Northeast, governors would not allow their state militias to join the national Army, and as Madison had feared, financiers refused to grant loans for the war effort. The war was the central issue in the presidential election of 1812; five out of six New England states voted for New York's DeWitt Clinton, but Madison won a second term.

Whether the War of 1812 was "the second war of American independence," as the war hawks claimed, or "Mr. Madison's War," as the Federalists chose to call it, was and is a matter of broad disagreement. While historian Bradford Perkins thinks that the President "seemed to drift rather than to direct policy" during the prelude to war, Irving Brant says that Madison encouraged the war movement in order to make his bid for peace from a position of strength, but that he was sabotaged by the Federalists, whose "active support of Great Britain and vituperation of their own government as . . . imbecile . . . created a dual delusion which poured on London in two lines of communi-

The Octagon House, above, was spared when the British burned Washington;
the Madisons lived there while the gutted White House was being restored.

cation." But however debatable his responsibility for the events of his first term, Madison was certainly not an effective Commander in Chief. No one commander was appointed to function as Washington had in the Revolution, and the various military operations were uncoordinated. In the summer of 1812, for instance, General William Hull marched boldly into Upper Canada, but realized too late that he might at any time be cut off at the Great Lakes by the British. Hurriedly retreating to Detroit, he waited for the British to besiege; they did, and on August 16 Hull surrendered his troops and the city to the enemy. When Buffalo fell the next year, American hopes of waging war principally on British soil were again dashed.

It was at sea, surprisingly, that America was most successful. Against the most formidable navy in the world, warships of the United States not only held their own in combat but frequently outmaneuvered their adversaries in matters of pure seamanship. If British complacency was shaken, American morale was boosted by several well-timed and widely quoted comments. "Now boys," said Captain Isaac Hull, "pour it into them," as his frigate *Constitution* battered the H.M.S. *Guerrière* into submission. "Old Ironsides" became the symbol of America's underdog sea strength, but even sinking ships sometimes left legacies of slogans: "Don't give up the ship!" said Captain James Lawrence as his *Chesapeake* went down with him aboard. And on September 10, 1813, Commodore Oliver Hazard Perry won the Battle of Lake Erie. "We have met the enemy and they are ours," he reported. When the British left Detroit, William Henry Harrison followed them into Canada and won the Battle of the Thames.

As American troops halted British advances in the Northwest, the war was stalemated. But in the summer of 1814, with Napoleon exiled to Elba, London was able to turn its full attention to America. In August, a company of British troops landed at Chesapeake Bay. After scattering the Americans at Bladensburg, Maryland, they proceeded to Washington.

On the morning of August 24, as the sound of cannon neared, Dolley Madison remained in the White House waiting for the President, who was at a meeting at the Navy yard. She spent the day looking through her spyglass, supervising the removal of Gilbert Stuart's portrait of George Washington, and writing a letter to her sister. In the afternoon she wrote: "Mr. Madison comes not; may God protect him! Two messengers covered with dust come to bid me fly; but I wait for him. . . ." Later, a note from Madison arrived, explaining that he had left the city and that she must do the same. Gathering up what silver she could, she fled to Virginia. Soon Washington was in flames.

The British then moved on to Baltimore, which is situated behind a hilly peninsula that creates a bottleneck in Chesapeake Bay. As the British ships sailed near the peninsula, they were held off by the guns of Fort McHenry and by a civilian army in the hills. Through the night of September 13 the British bombarded the fort. By dawn's early light, Francis Scott Key, aboard an American dispatch boat, noted that the flag was still there.

The battles at Baltimore and the American victory at Plattsburg, New York, strengthened the position of the American commission at Ghent, Belgium, where the belligerents were trying to negotiate settlement of an unnecessary war. On Christmas Eve, 1814, the Treaty of Ghent was signed, and the two nations returned to the prewar situation. American sea rights were not guaranteed, and Canada remained British. The last battle was waged after the peace had been made: on January 8, 1815, Jackson defeated the British at New Orleans.

James Madison emerged from the war with enhanced prestige and without political opposition. Regarded in the popular imagination as the little President who had tolerated no nonsense from the world's strongest empire, he was also thought of by Americans as the architect of victory even though neither side had won.

Warning Congress not to abruptly revoke all war measures, Madison abandoned his faithfulness to consistency. The author of the Virginia Resolutions, which asserted the rights of states, now denounced states' rights as subversive to the Constitution; and the onetime foe of the Bank of the United States decided, in 1816, to support its re-establishment. That same year, Madison signed a tariff bill of the kind he had once steadfastly opposed. There were, however, some limits to Madison's flexibility.

Although he went before Congress and urged the establishment of "a comprehensive system of roads and canals, such as will have the effect of drawing more closely together every part of our country," he vetoed an internal improvements bill. An amendment, he believed—not a bill—was needed.

At the end of his second term, in 1817, the Madisons returned to Montpelier, their Virginia home. There James Madison assumed the role of gentleman farmer, and Dolley continued playing hostess to the gentry. After several years in retirement, however, Madison again began taking active part in the affairs of his state and nation. In 1826, he succeeded Jefferson as rector of the University of Virginia. As a delegate to the Virginia Constitutional Convention of 1829 he protested the disproportionate power of the eastern slaveholders in the state legislature. Throughout Monroe's two terms, Madison wrote newspaper articles defending administration decisions and was a foreign policy adviser. He continued to work for the abolishment of slavery; he wrote his autobiography; and he rewrote his journal of the Constitutional Convention.

Madison's small body weakened, but his mind remained alert to the end. On June 27, 1836, he spent several hours dictating a letter. The next morning breakfast was brought to him in bed, but he could not swallow. When his niece asked him what was wrong, he replied, "Nothing more than a change of *mind*, my dear." And then, according to his servant, James Madison "ceased breathing as quietly as the snuff of a candle goes out."

In the House of Representatives, Congressman John Quincy Adams summarized James Madison's importance in American history: "Is it not in a pre-eminent degree by emanations from his mind, that we are assembled here as the representatives of the people and the states of this Union? Is it not transcendently by his exertions that we address each other here by the endearing appellation of countrymen and fellow-citizens?"

—VINCENT BURANELLI

James Madison

A PICTURE PORTFOLIO

*Presidential medals, such as this one depicting
Madison, were presented to Indian chieftains as
symbols of American friendship and good will.*

FATHER OF
THE CONSTITUTION

When James Madison arrived in Philadelphia for the Constitutional Convention of 1787, he had with him two original essays, "Vices of the Political System of the United States" and "Study of Ancient and Modern Confederacies." Although all the delegates acknowledged the inadequacies of the Articles of Confederation, they were sharply divided in their views on a strong federal government. Madison, armed with his two scholarly documents, presented example after example of nations gaining strength and longevity under a central authority, or faltering and dy-

The portrait above, by Gilbert Stuart, shows James Madison in his mid-fifties as Secretary of State under Thomas Jefferson, some sixteen years after the Constitution had been ratified. The sculpture by Lee Lawrie, at right, is entitled "Drafting the Constitution," and is part of a frieze at the State Capitol of Nebraska. Seated left to right are Benjamin Franklin, George Washington, and Alexander Hamilton; Madison is the fourth standing figure from the left, his coat partially obscured by Franklin's chair. Among the others are James Wilson, Elbridge Gerry, Edmund Randolph, Rufus King, Gouverneur Morris, and Roger Sherman. After some two months of initial deliberations, the Constitutional Convention adjourned on July 26, 1787, to allow a committee of detail to compose a first draft. From August 6 until September 10 the assembly examined the nascent Constitution. A committee of style polished the document, and on September 15, at six in the evening, the Convention was ready to vote. "On the question to agree to the Constitution, as amended," Madison recorded, "All the States ay." The document was signed two days later and ratified in 1788.

ing when confederation was subordinate to individual elements. But although Madison was probably the most effective advocate of a powerful federal government, it was his willingness to compromise that made him the "Father of the Constitution." Most of the great compromises that made ratification of the Constitution possible—the two legislative branches, the "federal ratio" (slaves were counted as three-fifths of a man) that helped maintain a balance in representation of Northern and Southern states, suffrage restrictions—were suggested by Madison, as were many of the checks and balances. He was equally effective in the effort to win ratification of the document, and in pressing for the adoption of the Bill of Rights. Madison served in the new nation's Congress for four terms, during which he organized the Antifederalists behind Jefferson as the Democratic-Republican party. In 1801, when the party won the Presidency, James Madison became Jefferson's Secretary of State. The obvious choice to succeed Jefferson in the White House, Madison beat Charles Cotesworth Pinckney easily, and on March 4, 1809, he took the oath of office as the nation's fourth President.

DOLLEY

When Dolley Madison made her entrance into Long's Hotel for the inaugural ball of 1809, characteristically dressed in pale velvet, plumed turban, and pearls, she confirmed a friend's earlier appraisal of her as "all dignity, grace and affability." More somber was her husband James, whose face already reflected the cares of his new office. Certainly not among those cares was the running of the White House: that was Dolley's bailiwick, as it had been when she was official hostess for widower Thomas Jefferson. Her cheerful informality had complemented Jefferson's domestic simplicity, but now that she was actually living in the manor to which she had become accustomed, Dolley intensified the social schedule. The First Lady's weekly receptions and "drawing rooms," her teas, lawn parties, and dinners, belied her Quaker upbringing, and a few detractors noted that Dolley took snuff and was "said to rouge"; but her career as a hostess and *grande dame*, spanning nearly half a century, was a spectacularly popular one. Her aplomb at White House functions often was a political asset to her reticent husband, and in crises she could display a cool common sense: among the few things she saved before the British burned the White House in 1814 were some vital state documents and Gilbert Stuart's portrait of George Washington. Dolley faithfully nursed James Madison through his retirement at Montpelier, and when he died in 1836, she became a widow for the second time (her first husband, John Todd, had died of yellow fever in 1793). Although financial troubles plagued her for the rest of her life, Dolley maintained her poise: as a contemporary described Dolley's extraordinary quality, "'Tis not her form, 'tis not her face, it is the woman altogether. . . ."

The daguerreotype above, attributed to Mathew Brady, was made on July 4, 1848. Dolley had returned to Washington in 1837 and had resumed her role as a leader of society in the Capital. Her last appearance was at a ball for James K. Polk in 1848; she died the following July, at the age of eighty-one.

The picture by Ezra Ames (left) captures the cheerful, almost puckish charm of Dolley in her prime.

145

RUNNING MATES AND RIVALS

LIBRARY OF CONGRESS

GEORGE CLINTON

When Vice President George Clinton voted against rechartering the Bank of the United States in 1811, he broke a Senate tie, thereby killing the measure and affirming an abiding animosity for President James Madison, who had supported the bill. Madison was angry but not surprised; the Vice President he had inherited from Jefferson had always been a thorn in his side. A staunch supporter of state sovereignty since the Revolution, Clinton had opposed ratification of the Constitution. Extremely popular with New York voters, he was elected governor of that state seven times. He was nominated as Jefferson's running mate in 1804 because he was a Republican in a normally Federalist state, but he disapproved of Jefferson's policies, and as the election of 1808 approached, he charged that Madison would "make our situation still worse if possible." The Republicans, not wishing to lose support in New York and expecting Clinton to refuse renomination because of his age (he was sixty-five in 1804), offered him the chance to run again—and he accepted. He then proceeded to campaign openly for the Presidency against Madison, but was re-elected Vice President. In April, 1812, after a long period of poor health, Clinton became the first Vice President of the United States to die in office.

INDEPENDENCE NATIONAL HISTORICAL PARK

ELBRIDGE GERRY

Both of James Madison's Vice Presidents died in office. Like George Clinton of the first administration, Elbridge Gerry was in his sixties when nominated and was considered valuable to the ticket because he was a popular Republican from a Federalist state. Born in Massachusetts in 1744 to a wealthy shipping family, Gerry was a follower of patriot Samuel Adams. After national independence had been won, his inconsistencies on political issues began to negate the value of his breeding, integrity, and willingness to work. He opposed the Constitution because of its departures from pure republicanism, yet supported Alexander Hamilton's Federalist financial policies. Sent to Paris in 1797, his lack of trust in his diplomatic colleagues and his excessive trust in Talleyrand helped sabotage the peace commission, and when he returned home he was snubbed by the Federalist war hawks and embraced by the pro-French Republicans. In 1810, while Massachusetts was still a Federalist stronghold, Gerry, running as a Republican, won the governorship. To help his party, he sponsored a bill that redistricted the state in such a way that each Republican state senator represented considerably fewer voters than each Federalist senator; this technique is now known as "gerrymandering."

CHARLES C. PINCKNEY

When Federalist Charles Cotesworth Pinckney was defeated by James Madison in the presidential election of 1808, it was the third time he had failed in a bid for national office. Nominated for the Vice Presidency in 1800 (although Alexander Hamilton had worked furtively for his election to the Presidency), Pinckney received 64 votes but finished behind Thomas Jefferson, Aaron Burr, and John Adams. In 1804, his party chose him to oppose Jefferson's all-but-certain re-election; Pinckney lost by a landslide, 162 votes to 14. Born in South Carolina and educated in England, Pinckney was a brigadier general during the Revolution, a member of the South Carolina legislature, and a prominent delegate to the Constitutional Convention. He declined President Washington's offer to appoint him commander of the Army, a Supreme Court justice, or Secretary of State or War; but he accepted the post of minister to France in 1796, during the early stages of the Franco-American crisis. The French Directory refused to receive him, but a year later he returned to Paris on a mission that culminated in the notorious XYZ Affair. Despite his three electoral defeats, Pinckney remained active in various public affairs until his death in Charleston in 1825.

DeWITT CLINTON

As a presidential candidate in the election of 1812, DeWitt Clinton, usually a master of the game of politics, overplayed his hand. Nominated by the prowar New York Republicans, he won the Federalist endorsement by representing himself as one who would end the war. His double-dealing caught up with him during the campaign, and he lost to Madison by an electoral vote of 128 to 89. A New Yorker, Clinton was elected to the state senate in 1798, when he was twenty-nine. Gaining control of the council of appointments, he advanced his career by use of the spoils system. He held the New York City mayoralty for ten of the twelve years between 1803 and 1815, during which time he supported public education and health facilities and took special interest in developing the shipping trade. In 1816 the state legislature approved the canal system he had long advocated; the following year he was elected governor. After two terms in Albany he retired, but he held the post of canals commissioner until political infighting led to his dismissal. In 1824, however, he was elected to the state house once again. Clinton therefore had the well-earned honor of presiding at the openings of both the Erie and Champlain canals. He died in Albany in 1828, at the age of fifty-eight.

AN UNWANTED WAR

It appears," wrote James Madison in April, 1812, that the British "prefer war with us to a repeal of their Orders in Council. We have nothing left therefore, but to make ready for it." During his three years as President, Madison had tried diplomatic persuasion, commercial restrictions, and even threats of war, to make England and France cease their harassment of American vessels and seamen. None of his efforts had succeeded, however, and now he concluded that war with Britain, with whom lay "the original sin against the neutrals," was the only solution. Madison was acutely aware of the national disunity which would hamper an effective war effort; he knew that the Treasury was inadequate and that the armed forces were deficient in both men and matériel. Observed South Carolina's John C. Calhoun: "He reluctantly gives up the system of peace." But in his war message of June 1, President Madison cited "evidence of hostile inflexibility in tramping on rights which no independent nation can relinquish." A bitterly divided Congress, urged on by expansion-minded Southerners and Westerners ("The militia of Kentucky are alone competent to place Montreal and Upper Canada at your feet," trumpeted Speaker of the House Henry Clay), agreed to war, which was formally declared by the President on June 19.

The U.S.S. Constitution *engaged and destroyed the English ship* Guerrière *on August 19, 1812 (above). In October, Americans took Queenston Heights during the Niagara campaign in Canada. But when New York's militiamen refused to reinforce the position, a British force (below) recaptured the prominence easily.*

WASHINGTON AFLAME

In the summer of 1814 a large British force struck at selected points along the Eastern seaboard to divert attention from the Northern campaign. Ordered to destroy whatever they could, General Robert Ross and Rear Admiral Sir George Cockburn sailed up the Patuxent River in mid-August, bent on sacking Washington in reprisal for the destruction of the Upper Canadian capital, York. Although outnumbered, the British rolled through Bladensburg, Maryland, on August 24, scattering the heterogeneous, ineptly led American force. President Madison, who had watched the debacle, retired to Virginia. At dusk, Ross and Cockburn led a raiding party of two hundred men into an undefended Washington. They set the House and Senate ablaze and, wrote Congressman Charles Jared Ingersoll of Pennsylvania, left "the Capitol wrapped in its winding sheet of fire." At the White House, the marauders feasted on food that Dolley Madison had left for American troops before she fled earlier that day; with Dolley's wine, the British drank the President's health, "for being such a good fellow as to leave us such a capital supper." Cockburn and his men took whatever souvenirs pleased them and then, according to an American witness, put the Executive Mansion to the torch "with the ruthless firebrand of the Red Savages of the wood." Only a violent thunderstorm prevented the total destruction of the White House. The desecration of the federal Capital united the country in wrath. In September, American victories at Fort McHenry and Plattsburg ended the British threat in the East and North; Andrew Jackson ended it in the South and West early in 1815.

In the British cartoon above, Americans and British both scorn President Madison's flight from Washington.

The walls of the White House (above) survived the fire the British set in 1814, but the inside was gutted.

The roof of the House of Representatives (below in an 1815 sketch) collapsed during the conflagration.

HEROES OF THE WAR OF 1812

ZEBULON PIKE

The American goal in the North during 1813 was to gain control of the Great Lakes, thus forcing the British to find more hazardous ways of getting supplies to the marauding Indians. A key figure in the reduction of England's power on Lake Ontario was Zebulon Pike, who during the first decade of the century had established himself as a military explorer. He had led expeditions to the headwaters of the Mississippi, Red, and Arkansas rivers, and had reconnoitered vast areas of the Southwest. (The Colorado peak that bears his name commemorates this period of Pike's life.) Cleared of charges associating him with Aaron Burr's scheme in 1807 to carve a Western empire, the New Jersey-born Pike rose to the rank of brigadier general. In April, 1813, Commodore Isaac Chauncey and Pike sailed from Sackets Harbor, New York, with 1,800 men, intending to destroy British ships at York (Toronto) prior to joining the main army for an attack on Fort George on the Niagara River. While leading the successful assault on York, Pike and thirty-eight others were killed when a British powder magazine exploded. But during the battle a thirty-gun English ship was burned, a sixteen-gun vessel was captured, and seven hundred British soldiers were taken prisoner. The capital of Upper Canada was in the hands of the Americans.

STEPHEN DECATUR

Stephen Decatur was born of seafarers, and his skill and bravado in three wars proved him worthy of his ancestry. Made an acting lieutenant in 1799, he served in the Caribbean during the undeclared naval hostilities with France. With two Mediterranean cruises behind him, he was given command of a ship in November, 1803, during the Tripolitan War. Decatur's cunning destruction of the captured American frigate, the *Philadelphia*, earned him a captaincy in 1804; he participated in the two bombardments of Tripoli in August of that year. His brilliance as a naval strategist was evincing itself, and his courage in combat won him widespread respect. Decatur's service in the War of 1812 was highlighted by his seizure of the *Macedonian*, pride of the English fleet, near Madeira. A few weeks after the Treaty of Ghent was signed, Decatur's *President* was pursued by four blockading English ships: he disabled one but surrendered to the others; later a court of inquiry found the surrender justified. In 1815, Decatur was instrumental in stopping demands for tribute by Algiers, Tunis, and Tripoli, and exacted payment from them for the damages they inflicted on American ships during the War of 1812. He served for almost five years on the Board of Navy Commissioners, and was mortally wounded in a duel in 1820.

OLIVER PERRY

In a little over three hours on September 10, 1813, Master Commandant Oliver Perry accomplished two major objectives: he substantially reduced the criticism of President Madison by those who felt that American war efforts in the North were ineffectual, and he wrote his name indelibly into American naval history. The ambitious Perry, who at twenty-eight already had a long record of creditable service, had been granted earlier that year his request for command of the forces on Lake Erie. When the British commander, Robert Barclay, briefly lifted his blockade of Perry's small fleet, Perry sailed into open water and pursued the enemy to its station at Amherstburg. Short of supplies, Barclay sailed out on September 9, and the next morning the two fleets engaged in battle. The United States flagship *Lawrence* was disabled, but Barclay suffered heavier losses, and the British were forced to capitulate. It was the first capture of an English fleet by the American Navy, and when Perry reported, "We have met the enemy and they are ours," he was an immediate hero. Control of the lake facilitated successful American campaigns in Canada, giving weight to United States territorial claims at Ghent. Perry went on to fight the British along the Potomac in 1814, and later held a command in the Mediterranean.

THOMAS MACDONOUGH

A year and a day after Oliver Perry's victory on Lake Erie, Master Commandant Thomas Macdonough engineered a parallel triumph on Lake Champlain. As in the earlier engagement, victory was due to the courage and tactical brilliance of the American commander. Macdonough was only sixteen when he became a midshipman in 1800. During the next ten years he rose through the ranks, serving tours of duty along the Atlantic coast, in the West Indies, and in the Mediterranean. When he was given command of the Lake Champlain forces in 1812, he was faced, as Perry had been, with building a fleet and gaining supremacy over the enemy on a crucial body of water. For two years, Macdonough was frustrated by shortages of men and matériel; the balance of power seesawed between his fleet and that of British Commodore George Downie. In late summer, 1814, Downie was supremely confident. But when the battle was joined on September 11 in Plattsburg Bay, Macdonough outmaneuvered the stronger British flagship and forced Downie's surrender. Deservedly lauded for his successful engagement, Macdonough continued his naval career with two more tours of duty in the Mediterranean. His health failed, however, and, in 1825, Thomas Macdonough died aboard a merchantman at forty-one.

"HUZZA HUZZA"

The Treaty of Ghent settled few of the issues over which the War of 1812 was fought: neither belligerent gained or lost territory, and American shipping rights were no more secure than they had been before the hostilities. Nevertheless, the citizens of the United States were jubilant, as the exultant kerchief at left indicates. The young nation's ships had held their own against—and had often beaten— the British navy, and Andrew Jackson's ragtag troops had routed "the conquerors of the conquerors of Europe" at New Orleans. The only real loser in the war was the Federalist party. Opposed to the conflict from the beginning, the New England Federalists had met in Hartford in 1814, where they had drafted a series of resolutions referring to the federal government in the second person and threatening secession. But news of the Treaty of Ghent arrived just as the Federalist delegation appeared in Washington to voice their dissent. "Their position," said French minister Louis Sérurier, "was awkward, embarrassing, and lent itself cruelly to ridicule." Federalism was not immediately replaced by another party; instead factionalism gave way to a surge of nationalism and, as Sérurier said, to the evolution of "a national character founded on a common glory for all." When James Madison retired to Virginia in 1817, he turned over to President James Monroe the leadership of a strong and proud United States, beginning an "era of good feelings."

FACTS IN SUMMARY: JAMES MADISON

CHRONOLOGY

UNITED STATES		MADISON				
	1751	*Born March 16*	Whisky Rebellion	1794	*Marries Dolley Todd*
Stamp Act	1765		Adams elected President	1796	
Virginia Resolves	1769	*Attends College of New Jersey (Princeton)*	Alien and Sedition Acts	1798	*Frames Virginia Resolutions*
First Continental Congress	1774	*Becomes member of Committee of Safety*	Undeclared naval war with France		
Lexington and Concord	1775		Jefferson inaugurated as President	1801	*Appointed Secretary of State by Jefferson*
Declaration of Independence	1776	*Attends Virginia Convention*	Tripolitan War		
		Elected to Virginia legislature	Marbury v. Madison	1803	
Articles of Confederation	1777		Louisiana Purchase		
	1778	*Elected to Virginia executive council*	Embargo Act passed	1807	
	1780	*Attends Continental Congress*		1808	*Elected President*
Yorktown	1781		Macon's Bill No. 2	1810	
	1784	*Elected to Virginia legislature*	West Florida annexed		
	1786	*Attends Annapolis Convention*	War of 1812 begins	1812	*Asks Congress for 60-day Embargo*
Constitutional Convention	1787	*Attends Continental Congress*	Surrender of Detroit		*Proclaims war with Great Britain*
		Attends Constitutional Convention	U.S. defeated in Canada		*Re-elected President*
Constitution ratified	1788	*Writes letters for* The Federalist	U.S. naval victories		
		Attends Virginia Ratification Convention	British blockade	1813	
Washington elected President	1789	*Elected to U.S. House of Representatives*	U.S. victories on Great Lakes and in Canada		
Bill of Rights			Creek War	1814	*Asks Congress to end Embargo*
			Washington burned		
			Hartford Convention		
			Treaty of Ghent		
			Battle of New Orleans	1815	*Vetoes bill for Second U.S. Bank*
			Second U.S. Bank created	1816	
			Monroe elected President		

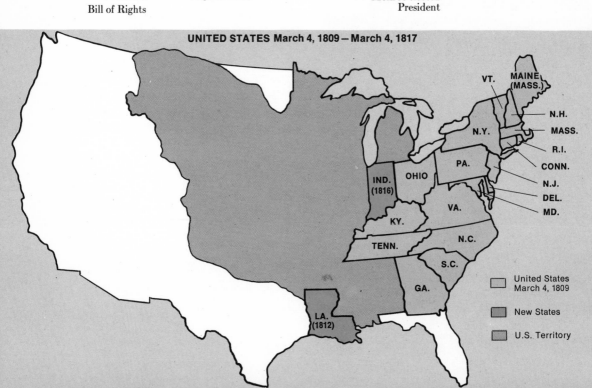

UNITED STATES March 4, 1809 — March 4, 1817

VT.
MAINE (MASS.)
N.H.
N.Y.
MASS.
R.I.
PA.
CONN.
IND. (1816)
OHIO
N.J.
DEL.
VA.
MD.
KY.
TENN.
N.C.
S.C.
GA.
LA. (1812)

☐ United States March 4, 1809
■ New States
■ U.S. Territory

	1817	*Vetoes bill for internal improvements*
		Retires to Montpelier
Missouri Compromise	1820	
	1826	*Becomes rector of University of Virginia*
Jackson elected President	1828	
	1829	*Delegate to Virginia Constitutional Convention*
Nullification Controversy	1832	
Siege of the Alamo	1836	*Dies June 28*

BIOGRAPHICAL FACTS

BIRTH: Port Conway, Va., March 16, 1751

ANCESTRY: English

FATHER: James Madison; b. March 27, 1723; d. Feb. 27, 1801

FATHER'S OCCUPATION: Justice of the peace; vestryman; farmer

MOTHER: Eleanor Conway Madison; b. 1732; d. Feb. 11, 1829

BROTHERS: Francis (1753–?); Ambrose (1755–1793); William (1762–1843); Reuben (1771–1775)

SISTERS: Nelly (1760–1802); Sarah (1761–?); Elizabeth (1768–1775); Frances (1771–?)

WIFE: Dorothea (Dolley) Payne Todd; b. Guilford County, N.C., May 20, 1768; d. Washington, D.C., July 12, 1849

MARRIAGE: Harewood, Va., Sept. 15, 1794

CHILDREN: None

HOME: Montpelier, Va.

EDUCATION: Received early education at Donald Robertson's school in Virginia and from private tutor; awarded A.B. from the College of New Jersey (Princeton) in 1771; one year postgraduate study at Princeton

RELIGIOUS AFFILIATION: Episcopalian

OCCUPATION BEFORE PRESIDENCY: Politician

PRE-PRESIDENTIAL OFFICES: Member of Orange County Committee of Safety; Delegate to the Virginia Convention; Member of Virginia Legislature; Member of Virginia Executive Council; Delegate to Continental Congress; Delegate to Annapolis Convention; Delegate to Constitutional Convention; Member of the Virginia Ratification Convention; U.S. Congressman; Secretary of State

AGE AT INAUGURATION: 57

DEATH: Montpelier, Va., June 28, 1836

PLACE OF BURIAL: Montpelier, Va.

ELECTION OF 1808

CANDIDATES	ELECTORAL VOTE
James Madison Democratic-Republican	122
Charles C. Pinckney Federalist	47
George Clinton Independent-Republican	6

FIRST ADMINISTRATION

INAUGURATION: March 4, 1809; House of Representatives, Washington, D.C.

VICE PRESIDENT: George Clinton

SECRETARY OF STATE: Robert Smith; James Monroe (from April 6, 1811)

SECRETARY OF THE TREASURY: Albert Gallatin

SECRETARY OF WAR: William Eustis; James Monroe (from Jan. 1, 1813); John Armstrong (from Feb. 5, 1813)

ATTORNEY GENERAL: Caesar Augustus Rodney; William Pinkney (from Jan. 6, 1812)

POSTMASTER GENERAL: Gideon Granger

SECRETARY OF THE NAVY: Robert Smith; Paul Hamilton (from May 15, 1809); William Jones (from Jan. 19, 1813)

SUPREME COURT APPOINTMENTS: Joseph Story (1811); Gabriel Duvall (1811)

ELEVENTH CONGRESS (March 4, 1809–March 4, 1811):
Senate: 28 Democratic-Republicans; 6 Federalists
House: 94 Democratic-Republicans; 48 Federalists

TWELFTH CONGRESS (March 4, 1811–March 4, 1813):
Senate: 30 Democratic-Republicans; 6 Federalists
House: 108 Democratic-Republicans; 36 Federalists

STATE ADMITTED: Louisiana (1812)

ELECTION OF 1812

CANDIDATES	ELECTORAL VOTE
James Madison Democratic-Republican	128
DeWitt Clinton Fusion	89

SECOND ADMINISTRATION

INAUGURATION: March 4, 1813; House of Representatives, Washington, D.C.

VICE PRESIDENT: Elbridge Gerry

SECRETARY OF STATE: James Monroe

SECRETARY OF THE TREASURY: Albert Gallatin; George W. Campbell (from Feb. 9, 1814); Alexander J. Dallas (from Oct. 14, 1814); William H. Crawford (from Oct. 22, 1816)

SECRETARY OF WAR: John Armstrong; James Monroe (from Oct. 1, 1814); William H. Crawford (from Aug. 8, 1815); George Graham (from Oct. 22, 1816)

ATTORNEY GENERAL: William Pinkney; Richard Rush (from Feb. 11, 1814)

POSTMASTER GENERAL: Gideon Granger; Return J. Meigs, Jr. (from April 11, 1814)

SECRETARY OF THE NAVY: William Jones; Benjamin W. Crowninshield (from Jan. 16, 1815)

THIRTEENTH CONGRESS (March 4, 1813–March 4, 1815):
Senate: 27 Democratic-Republicans; 9 Federalists
House: 112 Democratic-Republicans; 68 Federalists

FOURTEENTH CONGRESS (March 4, 1815–March 4, 1817):
Senate: 25 Democratic-Republicans; 11 Federalists
House: 117 Democratic-Republicans; 65 Federalists

JAMES MONROE

In May, 1817, two and a half months after he had become President, James Monroe left Washington for a tour of the Northern United States. Intending to inspect all the shipyards, forts, and frontier outposts for which Congress had voted large appropriations, he was also hopeful that his appearance would solidify national unity. Almost at once he discovered that the trip was succeeding beyond his hopes: roadsides and riverbanks were spotted with people anxious to have a glimpse of him, and cheering crowds greeted his arrival at state capitals. "In principal towns," he wrote to Thomas Jefferson, "the whole population has been in motion, and in a manner to produce the greatest degree of excitement possible."

After enjoying the receptions of the Middle Atlantic states, Monroe, perhaps bracing himself, entered New England, the last stronghold of federalism; the third consecutive Democratic-Republican President, he had lost Connecticut and Massachusetts in the election of 1816. But Monroe's doubts about the enthusiasm of the Yankees were soon dissipated. On July 12, 1817, the Boston *Columbian Centinel* noted Monroe's visit in this paragraph: "ERA OF GOOD FEELINGS . . . During the late Presidential Jubilee many persons have met at festive boards, in pleasant converse, whom party politics had long severed. We recur with pleasure to all the circumstances which attended the demonstration of good feelings."

Whether or not feelings were really good during the "Era of Good Feelings" is a matter of conjecture, but the label became fastened to the Monroe administration, and the President profited. His popularity extended from the masses to many old political adversaries—the *Columbian Centinel*, for example, which was a dogmatic, consistently Federalist newspaper and a traditional foe of the Democratic-Republicans. Once a devoted party man,

This portrait of Monroe was made around 1820 by Rembrandt Peale.

According to James Monroe's descendants, this liquor chest accompanied the President on his travels.

Monroe found himself the personification of nonpartisan paternalism, credited with all the good but rarely blamed for the ills of his two terms. Even John Quincy Adams—who rather than say anything nice about anybody could usually be counted on to say nothing at all—wrote that the Monroe years would "be looked back to as the golden age of this republic."

The times were just right for James Monroe to assume the Presidency. In his Inaugural Address he said, "the United States have flourished beyond example. Their citizens individually have been happy and the nation prosperous. . . . The sentiment in the mind of every citizen is national strength. It ought therefore to be cherished." Americans agreed: the success of their Revolution, of their experiment with republicanism, of their military engagements—most recently the War of 1812—had buoyed their spirits and bolstered their national pride, unity, and ambition. Now the young country was growing, and a nationalistic generation, born under the American flag, was confident it could handle the problems expansion would raise. Still, Americans looked for leadership and example to the fathers of their independence. Washington was dead, Adams and Jefferson were old, and Madison was stepping down;

but there was Monroe: if he had not forged the Revolution he had at least helped to wage it, and, besides, he looked the part. Not yet sixty, he stood tall, angular, erect, his features large and chiseled, his blue-gray eyes at once penetrating and kind, and from a short distance he bore an unmistakable resemblance to George Washington. Wearing no-longer-stylish pantaloons, powdering his iron-colored hair, dressing from time to time in his old military uniform, he filled the role well, knowing, as the people knew, that he was the last of the great eighteenth-century figures who would lead the nation.

The Monroes were landowning farmers, neither rich nor poor, not quite aristocratic but quite respectable in Virginia's complex hierarchy. James Monroe, oldest of five children, was born in Westmoreland County on April 28, 1758. He probably became a patriot at an early age, for his father was an admirer of Patrick Henry and an occasional petitioner for colonial causes, and his mother's brother, Judge Joseph Jones, was a friend to Washington, Jefferson, and Madison. With his neighbor and classmate John Marshall, future United States Chief Justice, Monroe walked several miles a day to and from the school of Parson Archibald Campbell, reputedly "a disciplinarian of the sternest type. . . ."

In 1774, at the age of sixteen, Monroe was sent to Williamsburg to acquire an education and a Virginia gentleman's polish at William and Mary College. Before the year was out, his father died, but Judge Jones paid the bills to keep Monroe in school. Neither time nor place, however, was conducive to scholarship. Then the capital of Virginia, Williamsburg was a center of colonial discontent, and local ears were tuned to Philadelphia, where the First Continental Congress had convened. Monroe began drilling with student-formed military companies, and in 1775 received a lieutenant's commission in the Third Virginia Regiment.

In August, 1776, Congress ordered a number of state infantries, the Virginia Third among them, to New York. By the time the Virginians arrived, the city had been lost to the British; General Washington was holed up at Harlem Heights. Most of Monroe's earliest experiences with the Continental Army were devoted to retreating, the successful defense of White Plains being an exception. As November brought winter down the Hudson, Washington took his fast-shrinking army across it, through New Jersey, and across the Delaware River into Pennsylvania. Despite the diminished condition of his troops and supplies, the General decided to recross the Delaware, hoping that the holiday merriment of his opponents would serve as an equalizer. On Christmas night, while the Hessian mercenaries who occupied Trenton slept the sleep of the intoxicated feaster, the Americans penetrated the city. It was daylight when the Hessians realized what was happening. As they mobilized, Monroe led a column of troops in a victorious race to the arsenal. During the action a ball struck his shoulder, hitting an artery, and he needed two months in bed to regain his strength. During his convalescence, spent in the Pennsylvania home of a judge named Wyncoop, he learned that Washington had promoted him to the rank of captain, and he fell in love with his host's daughter, who was already spoken for.

Monroe was not yet nineteen, and a captain, but enlistments were so few that there were not enough men for the formation of a company for him to command. In August, 1777, he became an aide to Lord Stirling, Major General William Alexander, the self-proclaimed "American Earl." On September 11, after the rout at Brandywine Creek, Monroe tended the wounds of the French officer Lafayette, and the two soldiers became lifetime friends. Then Monroe participated in the abortive American attack of Germantown and was promoted to major.

In 1779, when the war shifted south, Monroe returned home, anxious to defend his state. In one of his rare letters of recommendation, General Washington wrote to the Virginia legislature suggesting that the major be given a command in the militia. "In every instance," the General wrote, Monroe "maintained the reputation of a

brave, active, and sensible officer." Once again, however, he was a victim of the manpower shortage, and he received the commission but no company.

Advising Monroe to take advantage of the lull, Judge Jones suggested that he study with Thomas Jefferson, who, though he was then governor, still accepted a number of law students. Jones provided the introduction, the Washington letter provided the best of recommendations, and Monroe spent three years with the governor. They established a friendship that lasted until Jefferson's death in 1826.

It was easy to be friendly to James Monroe. "He is a man," said Jefferson, "whose soul might be turned wrong side outwards without discovering a blemish to the world." Straightforward, generous, not in the least pretentious, seldom discouraged for long, Monroe was trustworthy and trusting, and he had the ability to retain his friends even through profound political disagreements. Even his political limitations were often misplaced expressions of his personal qualities: he could be overgenerous, honest to the point of naïveté, and indiscreet.

He entered politics in 1782 as a member of the Virginia assembly and a year later was elected to the Continental Congress. In both state and national affairs he distinguished himself as a Jeffersonian agrarian-liberal, strongly sectionalist, a foe of centralized government, and a champion of frontier development. He made two trips "through the wilderness," and once seriously, though unofficially, suggested that the United States think about convincing Britain to relinquish Canada. As a member of the Virginia Convention of 1788, he originally opposed the Constitution on the grounds that it assigned too much power to the federal government. As for slavery, when a vote on some aspect of the issue came up, he absented himself.

Monroe ran for Congress in 1788 but was badly beaten by James Madison. In 1790, however, the Virginia legislature elected him to the United States Senate. During his four years in the Senate he was—with Jefferson's advice, Madison's cooperation, and Aaron

Monroe purchased these dueling pistols in Spain.

Burr's political expertise—instrumental in organizing opposition to the policies and philosophy of Alexander Hamilton. The result was a consolidation of Antifederalist factions that became the Democratic-Republican party.

In 1794 relations between the United States and France were beginning to worsen. Gouverneur Morris, the American minister to France, was a Federalist of aristocratic inclinations, hardly sympathetic to revolutionary France, whose government demanded his recall. Moreover, John Jay was in England negotiating a treaty, and the French were upset lest the United States become allied to Great Britain. To soothe the French, President Washington appointed a Republican minister, Monroe.

When he arrived in Paris, Monroe addressed the National Convention. Calling France "our ally and friend," he praised "the fortitude, magnanimity and heroic valor of her troops . . . the wisdom and firmness of her councils," and assured his audience that Jay would not weaken the relationship between the United States and France.

Across the Channel, the English read of Monroe's laudatory speech and found it disagreeable. Washington thought it not "well devised," and Secretary of State Edmund Randolph wrote the minister, reminding him to cultivate French friendship "with zeal, proportioned to the value we set upon it." Then, late in 1794, Monroe managed to secure the release of Thomas Paine, long a thorn in Washington's side, from prison, where he had been confined by extremists for his opposition to the execution of the King during the French Revolution. Paine soon launched an attack on the American President, who could not have been pleased by Monroe's generosity to the patriot.

But Monroe's usefulness was gone anyway. The French were angered by the terms of Jay's Treaty, and the American minister obviously sided with the French. President Washington felt that a minister's responsibility was to defend his government's policy, and in December of 1796 Monroe was recalled. When he returned home, Monroe demanded without success that Washington make public the reasons for his recall and wrote a vindictive, damning attack on the General. It was not published until December, 1797, when John Adams was President. Adams employed the treatise in his propaganda campaign against the French, reminding Americans that the fine send-off the French had given "a disgraced minister, recalled in displeasure for misconduct, was a studied insult to the government of my country." Actually Monroe had been recalled for the good reason that his performance had been inconsistent with the position of the government he represented. But he kept the issue alive, published the unfortunate paper, and gave ammunition to the Federalists.

Monroe recovered. National sentiment was increasingly Republican, and he found that the French experience had gained him more in recognition than it had cost him in popularity. Washington, however, remained bitter—not without cause—about Monroe's attack. One December night in 1799, he returned home from a walk in the snow and was informed that James Monroe had just been elected governor of Virginia. Without changing his wet clothes, he sat before the fire and angrily discussed the news and his ex-soldier's ungrateful treachery. The snow on his apparel melted; he developed chills and the infection that led to his death.

In 1803 Monroe agreed to give diplomacy another try when President Jefferson asked him to return to France to engineer a treaty for free navigation of the Mississippi River. Before Monroe arrived in Paris, however, Robert Livingston negotiated the Louisiana Purchase, and Monroe was directed to Madrid to acquire Spanish Florida. When Spain refused to sell, Jefferson instructed him to go to London to see what could be done about ending Anglo-American tensions over shipping. On December 31, 1806, a treaty was signed, but since it made no reference to American rights on the high seas, the government disavowed it. Noting Monroe's record in the foreign service, Jefferson thought this an opportune moment to offer Monroe the governorship of the Louisiana Territory, "the second office in the United States in importance." Monroe refused and returned home in 1807. The next year, when James Madison was elected President, Monroe hoped for a Cabinet post, but was once again offered the governorship of Louisiana, which he did not want, and he returned to Virginia.

James Monroe's career resumed in 1810, when he was elected to the Virginia legislature, and from then on it virtually galloped to the Presidency. In 1811 he again became governor, but less than three months after taking office, he was asked to become Secretary of State, replacing Robert Smith. Smith had left the Department of State in chaos, and Monroe revealed his splendid administrative skills by creating an orderly, smooth-functioning agency. In 1814, during the war with England, Monroe also took charge of the disorganized Department of War, thus assuming a dual role in the Madison Cabinet. As Secretary of War, he built another well-oiled machine. The tide of war turned, and he became the most prestigious and logical Republican to receive the presiden-

DANIEL TOMPKINS

Daniel D. Tompkins seemed the ideal choice as James Monroe's running mate in 1816: the popular young governor of New York was a faithful Republican who had worked for improvements in educational facilities, a reformed penal code, and the abolition of slavery. The Monroe ticket won, but Tompkins had a difficult time during his tenure as Vice President. While governor of New York, during the War of 1812, he had accepted the command of the Third Military District and had secured badly needed loans (largely on personal credit) for both the New York and federal governments. But he had failed to keep accurate records of his transactions, and both governments claimed that he was heavily in debt to them. In 1821, New York settled the matter by declaring that Tompkins owed the state nothing and vice versa. The federal government took no action except to withhold his annual vice presidential salary of $5,000. Tompkins ran unsuccessfully for a fifth term as governor of New York in 1820, the same year in which he was re-elected Vice President. Depressed by his long campaign of self-vindication, he began to drink heavily and left Washington more than two years before the end of his second term. In 1824, Congress paid him $95,000, although he claimed he was owed $660,000. This "most injured of all men," as Martin Van Buren referred to Daniel Tompkins, died at the age of fifty in 1825.

tial nomination in 1816. The faltering Federalists were hardly a threat. Monroe won 183 electoral votes to 34 for Rufus King.

After his thirteen-state good-will tour, Monroe and his wife settled into the White House, which had been restored after the British had burned it in 1814. Monroe had married Elizabeth Kortright of New York in 1786. As First Lady she was quite a contrast to her spirited predecessor: whereas Dolley Madison had skipped about Washington paying social calls, Mrs. Monroe stayed at home, and the Capital's ladies came to her. Not that Elizabeth Monroe was antisocial—she was just formal. The spontaneity of Dolley's parties was replaced by the grandeur of Elizabeth's lavish dinners and balls.

Expansion was the prevailing issue of the Monroe administration, and expansion, of course, inspired or brought to the surface of government a number of greater issues. A nation could not simply annex territory. A nation first had to discover which land was its own and which was not; borders had to be defined; the development of new areas had to be planned; policies regarding foreign rights to neighboring territory had to be established. And the American nation had its own unique problem—slavery—to deal with: which, if any, annexed territory should be slave, and which, if any, free?

On the question of slavery, Monroe himself mirrored the paradox of the nation. Like most humanitarians, he opposed the institution, yet he owned slaves. He supported the American Colonization Society, which favored the establishment of a colony in the African state of Liberia to which American slaves would be deported. (Liberia liked the idea and named its capital, Monrovia, after the President.) American intellectuals of the time seldom considered the possibility of racial integration in the United States and chose to keep slaves and treat them well rather than release them into a society into which they could not become assimilated.

In 1819, when Missouri applied for admission to the Union, there were eleven slave states and eleven free states in the country. One way or another, the admission of Missouri would destroy this balance. Naturally, the North wanted Missouri admitted free, and the South, slave; the debates were ferocious. "I have never known a question so menacing to the tranquillity and even the continuance of our Union as the present one," Monroe wrote.

Another not-quite-forgotten issue that expansion fostered was that of internal improvements. A growing United States needed post offices, an interstate highway system, canals, and conservation programs. Like Jefferson and Madison, Monroe was emphatically in favor of federal legislation for the advancement of internal improvements, but he was also certain that the Constitution gave the government no such legislative powers. During his Northern trip in 1817, he thought he came up with a constitutional course to pursue: acting as Commander in Chief, he ordered the Department of War to repair a number of damaged roads in New York, claiming that maintenance of the roads was essential to national defense. Henry Clay of Kentucky, also an advocate of internal improvements, opposed congressional appropriation of the funds on the reasonable grounds that this was a roundabout method of handling a problem that required direct federal action. The President, however, having failed to convince Congress that a constitutional amendment should be passed, decided that he would have to veto bills for internal improvements.

And there was the problem of foreign policy. The United States was growing by leaps and bounds; how large it would ultimately get was becoming clearer: Americans were beginning to look to the wilderness between the Mississippi and the Pacific, but the definition of North-South borders was fuzzy. In 1817 Monroe dispatched a team of negotiators to London to settle the United States-Canada border, and the Convention of 1818 was arranged. The boundary was established along the forty-ninth parallel to the Rockies, beyond which was the Oregon Territory, where Americans and Canadians would enjoy equal rights. In the South, America wanted Spanish Florida to round off its Atlantic

coastline. In 1818 General Andrew Jackson and his men roamed at will through the Spanish possession. Madrid got the message. With the Spanish minister to Washington, Luis de Onís, Secretary of State John Quincy Adams worked out the details, and the Adams-Onís Treaty of 1819 added all of Florida to the United States.

Finally, in that same year, the Bank of the United States, established in 1816, failed, triggering the Panic of 1819 and a depression that lasted several years. Coming as it did the year before an election, the Panic could have been a great threat to Monroe's desire for a second term, but it was not. He was, after all, the symbol of the Era of Good Feelings. The ruined, the dispossessed and unemployed, blamed instead the symbol of finance. The Bank, which did not have to stand for public office, became the object of public fury. Monroe was not even opposed. The Federalists were still around, but on their last legs, and could not muster strength enough to put up a candidate. Except for one dissenting ballot cast to ensure George Washington's place in American history as the only President to win unanimously, Monroe would have received all the votes.

The issues of his first administration continued—in most cases were magnified—during the second. Two of the results were the Missouri Compromise, which Jefferson called "the death knell of the Union," and the Monroe Doctrine.

On March 3, 1820, Congress had passed a compromise bill whereby Missouri would be admitted as a slave state, Maine would be admitted as a free state (thereby maintaining

Fort Ross, built in northern California by the Russians in 1812, was one of the reasons for the formulation of the Monroe Doctrine eleven years later.

the balance), and slavery would be barred from the territories of the Louisiana Purchase north of latitude 36°30′. After the bill had been signed by the President, but before the official admission date of Missouri, the Missouri legislature itself revived the seemingly settled issue by passing a law excluding free Negroes from the would-be state. Outraged, antislavery factions wanted to abrogate Missouri's admission. In his first triumph as "the Great Compromiser," Speaker of the House Henry Clay came up with a solution: until the Missouri legislature gave assurance that it would not deny rights to any American citizen, statehood would remain suspended. The Compromise merely prohibited Missouri from passing any law contrary to the Constitution, and naturally Missouri agreed.

President Monroe did not miss the ambiguity of the wording of the Missouri Compromise; nor did the fact that it had accomplished less than it had postponed escape him. But he was genuinely puzzled by the constitutional questions that had been raised. First, the Constitution acknowledged slavery; it may not have favored it, but by declaring (for purposes of apportionment) each slave equal to three-fifths of a man, it recognized the existence of the institution. Second, in Monroe's opinion, Congress did not have the right to restrict slavery in any state, as slavery was a local issue. But Congress did have the right to admit or deny admis-

165

sion to any territory. In short, the Constitution provided no clear answer. With the advice of his Cabinet he signed the Compromise, perhaps agreeing with John Quincy Adams, who, though he had advised the President to sign, said, "I take it for granted that the present question is a mere preamble—a titlepage to a great, tragic volume."

Monroe never really settled the question of internal improvements. He sincerely believed that the government ought to provide for them, but when the House passed an internal improvements bill in 1822, he vetoed it because he thought Congress had no power to so legislate under the Constitution. His successor, John Quincy Adams, would face the problem in reverse: he wanted the improvements made, claiming that the Constitution implied the necessary power to Congress, but by then Congress would not pass the improvements bill.

The question of European activity in the Americas first came up in the Monroe administration in 1821, when the Czar announced that he was extending Russia's Alaska territory down the Pacific coast of North America to the fifty-first parallel, which was located well within the Oregon Territory. Monroe immediately took the issue to his Cabinet and found Secretary of State Adams' words most agreeable. Adams said that "we should contest the right of Russia to *any* territorial establishment on this continent, and that we should assume distinctly the principle that the American continents are no longer subjects for *any* new European colonial establishments." After the President ordered a protest lodged in St. Petersburg, the Czar proved conciliatory and agreed to withdraw north of the territory, to the parallel of 54°40'.

Adams was also the architect of United States policy toward Latin America. Spain had bungled its attempts at colonization there and had lost, through revolutions, most of its American territories. In 1822 rumors were circulating that the Spanish, with French aid, were seriously considering the possibility of re-entering their lost colonies and recapturing the governments. Great Britain, anxious as ever to slap French hands, suggested that England and America publish a joint statement in support of the Latin countries, but Adams objected. "It would be more candid," he argued, "as well as more dignified, to avow our principles explicitly . . . than to come in as a cockboat in the wake of the British man-of-war."

Thus the Monroe Doctrine, written by Adams but made United States policy by James Monroe: "The American continents, by the free and independent condition which they have assumed and maintain, are henceforth not to be considered as subjects for future colonization by any European powers." Monroe drew the words from one of Adams' state papers and included them in his seventh annual message to Congress, on December 2, 1823. Although the Doctrine is only one sentence long, its implications have been gigantic. It has been employed as justification for a broad range of American actions—from the Spanish-American War to the Cuban Missile Crisis.

At the end of the Monroe administration the Marquis de Lafayette, after forty years' absence, returned for a visit to the United States. The reunion between the President and the foreign soldier who had become an American hero was moving, and the two men spent as much time as possible together during the next year. They said farewell on August 9, 1825, at a banquet given by the now ex-President.

Monroe retired to Oak Hill, his home in Loudoun County designed by architect Thomas Jefferson. In 1829 he returned to public service, becoming presiding officer of the Virginia Constitutional Convention. He led a battle for fair apportionment of legislative representation, opposed enlargement of the suffrage, and, once again, by and large avoided involvement with the slavery issue.

After Elizabeth died in 1830, Monroe, ailing and in financial difficulty stemming from his Presidency, sold Oak Hill and moved to New York to live with his daughter. He died there in 1831, the third of the nation's Presidents to die on the Fourth of July.

—DAVID JACOBS

James Monroe

A PICTURE PORTFOLIO

*This commemorative spoon honors the Monroe
Doctrine and the President who proclaimed it.*

When James Monroe was about twenty-four, he sat for the portrait at left by a now-forgotten artist. At that time, Monroe was a practicing attorney in Virginia.

In the painting at right, Monroe and Robert R. Livingston are shown purchasing Louisiana from Talleyrand.

In October, 1777, Monroe participated in the Battle of Germantown, depicted below in an 1850 painting by George Washington Parke Custis. General Washington, Monroe later recalled, took the British by surprise, and they were "driven before him." Although the Americans came close to victory, a morning fog confused the troops, and Washington was compelled to order them to retreat.

A CHECKERED CAREER

In spite of his diplomatic blunders abroad, James Monroe's political career flourished at home. Two reasons for his domestic successes were his extraordinary administrative skills and his fortunate friendships. During the Presidency of Washington (under whom he had served during the Revolution), Monroe was recalled from France in disgrace for having contradicted the policies of the administration he represented. But Jefferson, Monroe's mentor, and Madison, his friend, had organized the Democratic-Republican party, and Monroe's return to a well-established opposition party lessened the blow, making his recall seem a purely political matter. In 1799 Monroe was elected governor of Virginia, but in 1803 he failed again on a diplomatic mission abroad. Re-elected governor in 1811, he was called to Washington by Madison, whose Department of State was in chaos. Monroe straightened out the State Department, and with his organizational and supervisory abilities he also brought order to the War Department during the hostilities with England. His reward was the Presidency in 1817.

Entertainment at the White House during Monroe's Presidency was lavish and varied, befitting the Era of Good Feelings. On Inauguration Day, March 4, 1817, the band played a specially composed march that achieved some popularity, as evidenced by the sheet music pictured at left.

In 1821, sixteen Western Indians—"part of them all but naked," according to John Quincy Adams—were invited to the White House to stage a war dance for President Monroe and his guests. As Baroness Hyde de Neuville, wife of the French minister, watched, she drew the sketch below.

ERA OF
GOOD FEELINGS

The election of 1816 was hardly a contest. By its opposition to the War of 1812, the Federalist party had wrecked its future and the chances of its candidate, Rufus King. Both William H. Crawford and James Monroe had supporters among the Democratic-Republicans, but Monroe's record during the war, as Secretary of the Departments of War and State simultaneously, was enough to secure the party's nomination. Winning the election itself was much simpler. King received only the electoral votes of the die-hard Federalist states, Massachusetts, Delaware, and Connecticut, losing even his own New York and all others to Monroe. The final tally was 183 electoral votes to 34. Then even the die-hard states moved into the Monroe camp. With prosperity high, and expansion and nationalism prevailing, it was difficult to fault the Chief Executive; the years of the Monroe administration were known as the Era of Good Feelings, a name coined in Federalist Massachusetts. There were, however, some bad feelings too: the voteless common man was beginning to resent the governing class; the free states and the slave states were finding less to like about each other; the prosperity was unstable and threatened to end at any moment. But none of this, in the people's eyes, had anything to do with the President. He would have been unanimously reelected in 1820 had not one elector wanted to preserve that honor for Washington.

RUFUS KING

The two presidential candidates in 1816 were in many ways the antithesis of each other. While Monroe was an efficient executive nominated by a prospering political party with the momentum of four successful electoral victories behind it, Rufus King, senator from New York, was a brilliant orator—"he is unequalled," Daniel Webster said—endorsed by a dying party. In contrast to Monroe's poor record in the field of diplomacy, King served as United States minister to Great Britain from 1796 to 1803, and has been called one of the most effective ambassadors the nation has ever had. A Harvard graduate, Rufus King was a congressman from Massachusetts before moving to New York; at the Constitutional Convention and then in the United States Senate, he was an eloquent spokesman for federalism. After being defeated as the Federalist vice presidential candidate in 1804, he retired to his Long Island home. Four years later he tried again for the same office and lost. King was vigorously opposed to the War of 1812, and in 1813 returned to the Senate to lead the opposition—an opposition, as it turned out, that destroyed the Federalist party; he was its last presidential candidate. Remaining in Congress, King turned his eloquence against the institution of slavery, proposing a plan for the resettlement of freed Negroes. In 1825, President Adams appointed him minister to England. But he soon became ill and had to return home, where he died in 1827.

A FORMAL FAMILY

An unfamiliar tenant named protocol moved into the White House in 1817, and informality was evicted. The First Family was not "at home" to the casual visitor, and the First Lady did not return calls as her predecessors had. Seldom responsive to invitations, the Monroes often sent their oldest daughter, Eliza Hay, and her husband to represent them at banquets and embassy balls. Educated in Paris, the classmate of princesses, Eliza was herself largely responsible for all the Old World formality; but to Secretary of State Adams she was just an obstructive and "obstinate little firebrand" carrying on a "senseless war of etiquette." Before long angry Washington wives turned Mrs. Monroe's receptions into predominantly stag affairs. Eliza even involved her sixteen-year-old sister's wedding in her feud. Maria Hester Monroe's 1820 marriage to Samuel Gouverneur was the first White House wedding. Eliza, in charge of the arrangements, announced a "New York style" wedding; only the family and intimate friends of the Monroes were invited. Lacking precedent, the Russian minister politely inquired how he might acknowledge the marriage of the President's daughter. The diplomatic corps, Eliza replied brusquely, were to ignore it. Thus did the social-minded Eliza Hay rudely reject the opportunity to establish a "Washington style" wedding.

Badly burned by the British during the War of 1812, the Executive Mansion had been restored adequately enough for the Monroes to move in in 1817. Congress appropriated $50,000 to buy new furnishings for the Mansion, above, which was still unfinished and without porticoes when the Monroes left it in 1825.

The Monroes brought to the Executive Mansion many of the furnishings they had purchased during diplomatic missions to Europe. A figurine of Hannibal adorns the gilt-bronze clock above. The chair below once belonged to Marie Antoinette.

It is possible that Elizabeth Kortright Monroe (above) was almost as snobbish as people said she was. Stately and reserved, she was a regal First Lady, a grande dame who tried to make the White House a grandiose court. But Mrs. Monroe also had great courage and a fighting spirit. An aristocrat, she nevertheless married a hard-drinking Republican and made a good marriage. She repeatedly overcame chronic poor health to travel with him during his ambassadorial years. In 1794, while in France, she gained permission to see the imprisoned wife of the Marquis de La-fayette on the day of her scheduled execution; Mrs. Monroe's interest may have helped secure the Marchioness' release the next day. Elizabeth also enjoyed being an innovator: in 1807 she dressed her daughter in French pantalettes and thus introduced the garment to an amazed Capital.

This enamel miniature of Clay was worn as a pin.

THE GREAT COMPROMISER

Speaker of the House Henry Clay did not design the Missouri Compromise of 1820, but because his efforts on its behalf were the primary reason for its passage, he became known, thereafter, as America's "Great Compromiser." It was a role for which the Kentuckian was well suited: he had an instinctive dislike for extremist positions, which he referred to as "entirely too ultra." Shrewd, realistic, and cynical, Clay was also optimistic and ever conscious of the odds. Once, when a woman offered Lucretia Clay sympathy because of her husband's penchant for gambling, Mrs. Clay replied, "he usually wins."

Clay did not win every hand, but he won enough to remain an active player in national politics for four decades. Born in Virginia in 1777, the tall, ungainly lawyer moved to Lexington, Kentucky, at the age of twenty. Specializing in criminal law, he attracted state-wide attention because, according to local lore, he never lost a client to the hangman. He received his first taste of national politics in the first decade of the nineteenth century when, as a state legislator, he was twice appointed to fill unexpired terms in the United States Senate. After running successfully for Congress in 1810, he became a "war hawk" and Speaker of the House in the Madison administration. He also served on the peace commission that concluded the War of 1812. In 1817, he was eager to be Secretary of State under Monroe. When John Quincy Adams received the appointment, Clay vengefully refused to allow the inauguration to take place in the House.

Although he was a slaveowner, Clay believed in a strong Union. His "American System," which he advocated throughout most of his career, was based on a broad interpretation of the federal government's constitutional powers. Ironically, the most bitterly opposed aspects of the system—a protective tariff and a national bank—met with considerable success, while the more widely admired internal improvements provision was never passed as a whole because many doubted that the national government had the right to appropriate money for roads, canals, and land development. President Monroe signed a watered-down version of the bill, and John Quincy Adams sponsored, without success, a constitutional amendment permitting internal improvements.

Clay was a perennial candidate for the Presidency. After finishing last in a four-man field in 1824, he threw his support to Adams, who won and subsequently appointed him Secretary of State. Elected to the Senate in 1831, Clay ran for President as an anti-Jackson National Republican a year later and was badly beaten. He sought the Whig party nomination in 1840, 1844, and 1848, receiving it in 1844 and losing narrowly to James K. Polk. In 1849, after a year's retirement in Kentucky, he saw the clouds of disunion forming again, and he returned to the Senate where he sponsored the Compromise of 1850. Clay died in 1852 at the age of sixty-five, believing that the Union had been preserved; he was spared the knowledge that nothing at all had been resolved by his compromises.

A FAMOUS DOCTRINE

The Monroe Doctrine has become the most famous of American foreign policy statements, but for many years after it was proclaimed in 1823, it was regarded as almost meaningless by other nations. There would be, President Monroe stated in Secretary of State John Quincy Adams' words, no "future colonization by any European powers" in the Western Hemisphere. America would stay out of Europe's wars, and Europe would be expected to keep out of American affairs. But these declarations of policy were made by the leader of a young, relatively weak nation, and it was the British navy, not the Monroe Doctrine, that made other European powers wary of molesting South America. In the 1830's and 1840's, England and France made incursions in Latin America, but there was no mention of the Doctrine by the United States government. Not until the end of the nineteenth century, when American strength had grown to formidable proportions, did the Monroe Doctrine become a meaningful policy. That adherence to the nonintervention clause was discarded in 1917 is evidence that the Doctrine is no more inflexible than any good foreign policy. As for the nations of Latin America, the promise of United States protection was not long applauded. At first, many doubted that the United States could or would come to their aid in the event of an attack. Later, they wondered who would protect them from the United States.

CULVER PICTURES

Theodore Roosevelt blended a generous portion of Monroe Doctrine into his "big stick" soup. The nutritional quality of the mixture is explained in this 1901 cartoon, in which Uncle Sam Rooster shelters the Latin chicks.

Franklin Delano Roosevelt's Good Neighbor Policy greatly improved United States relations with Latin America: trade was increased, and many American military bases were withdrawn. But as Hitler and Mussolini gobbled up one nation after another in Europe, the possibility that they might turn next to the Americas was anything but remote. As the cartoon at left, published in July, 1940, shows, the United States waved the Monroe Doctrine to remind them that aggression in the Western Hemisphere would never be tolerated.

The press was lavish in its references to the Monroe Doctrine during the Cuban Missile Crisis of 1962, when President John F. Kennedy reaffirmed it in spirit if not in name.

FACTS IN SUMMARY: JAMES MONROE

CHRONOLOGY

UNITED STATES		MONROE
	1758	Born April 28
Lexington and Concord	1775	Leaves William and Mary to join army
Bunker Hill		
Declaration of Independence	1776	Promoted to first lieutenant
Battle of Trenton		Wounded at Trenton
		Promoted to captain
Articles of Confederation adopted	1777	Fights at Brandywine and Germantown
	1778	Fights at Monmouth
	1780	Appointed military commissioner of Southern army
		Studies law under Jefferson
	1782	Elected to Virginia House of Delegates
	1783	Elected to Continental Congress
Shays' Rebellion	1786	Admitted to the bar
		Marries Elizabeth Kortright
		Elected to Virginia assembly
Constitutional Convention	1787	
	1788	Elected to Virginia State Convention
		Defeated in election for congressman
Washington elected President	1789	

		MONROE
	1790	Elected to U.S. Senate
Jay's Treaty	1794	Appointed minister to France
John Adams elected President	1796	Recalled from France
	1799	Elected governor of Virginia
Jefferson elected President	1801	
Louisiana Purchase	1803	Participates in purchase of Louisiana Territory
		Appointed minister to England
	1804	Heads diplomatic mission to Spain
Monroe-Pinkney Treaty	1806	Appointed commissioner to negotiate treaty with England
Jefferson refuses to send Monroe-Pinkney Treaty to Senate	1807	Returns to America
Madison elected President	1808	
	1810	Elected to Virginia assembly
	1811	Elected governor of Virginia
		Appointed Secretary of State
War with Britain	1812	
Treaty of Ghent	1814	Appointed Secretary of War
	1816	Elected President

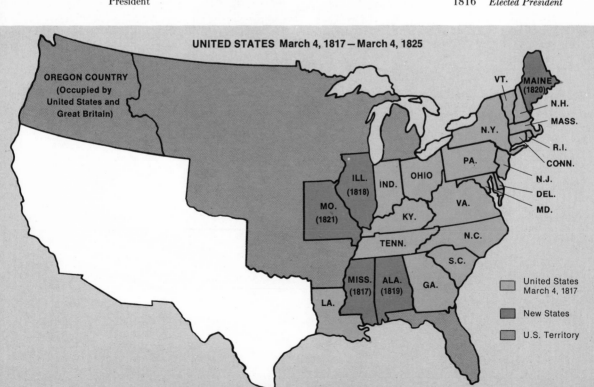

UNITED STATES March 4, 1817 — March 4, 1825

OREGON COUNTRY (Occupied by United States and Great Britain)

VT. · MAINE (1820) · N.H. · MASS. · N.Y. · R.I. · CONN. · PA. · N.J. · DEL. · MD. · ILL. (1818) · IND. · OHIO · MO. (1821) · KY. · VA. · TENN. · N.C. · S.C. · MISS. (1817) · ALA. (1819) · GA. · LA.

United States March 4, 1817

New States

U.S. Territory

A *preview of*
VOLUME 3

In the next volume are the life stories of John Quincy Adams, who was accused of making a "corrupt bargain" to win the Presidency; of Andrew Jackson, the hero of the Battle of New Orleans, who became "the People's President"; and of Martin Van Buren, the "Little Magician."

3

THE AMERICAN HERITAGE BOOK OF THE PRESIDENTS AND FAMOUS AMERICANS

General Andrew Jackson

The Battle of New Orleans

John Quincy Adams

DELL

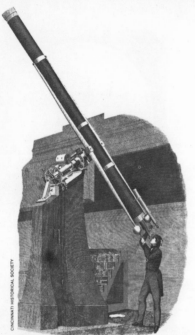

*An Ohio observatory, dedicated
by John Quincy Adams in 1843*

A campaign item of 1828

Admirers gave Jackson a 1,400-pound cheese.

1.

"In the East Room [of the White House], the mob hurled itself on the refreshments; to the sound of crystal breaking and china smashing, women fainted, fights erupted—noses, clothing, and furniture were bloodied." What event does that quotation describe?

2.

Which President was accused by a congressman of sleeping in a Louis XV bed, using perfume, and employing "gold-framed mirrors 'as big as a barn door' to behold his plain Republican self"?

3.

Who was the only man to resign from the Vice Presidency of the United States?

4.

"Do they think that I am such a damned fool as to think myself fit for President of the United States? No, sir; I know what I am fit for. I can command a body of men in a rough way; but I am not fit to be President." Which future President made that remarkably modest statement?

5.

Who was the only former President of the United States to serve in the House of Representatives after his term as Chief Executive was over?

6.

Which senator, whom Andrew Jackson had once attacked with a horsewhip, became his staunch ally in later years?

7.

The expression "O.K." was first used to refer to a President whose nickname was Old Kinderhook. Who was the President?

8.

What great battle of the War of 1812 took place *after* peace had been declared? Why?

9.

Which American diplomat, later elected President, found Henry Clay "dogmatical" and "over-bearing" and objected to his gambling and late hours?

Congress issued this Jackson medal.

Seminole attack a fort in Florida.

Van Buren is shown in the star below.

ANSWERS: 1. Andrew Jackson's inaugural reception at the White House in 1829 2. Martin Van Buren 3. John Caldwell Calhoun, in 1832 4. General Andrew Jackson, in 1821 5. John Quincy Adams 6. Thomas Hart Benton of Missouri 7. Martin Van Buren 8. The Battle of New Orleans, which took place on January 8, 1815, before word of the peace treaty signed in Europe reached Jackson 9. John Quincy Adams, who served with Clay on the commission negotiating the Treaty of Ghent in 1814

FAMOUS AMERICANS

Included in Volume 3 are Vice President Richard M. Johnson, who allegedly killed the Indian chief Tecumseh at the Battle of the Thames; Horace Mann and Mary Lyon, pioneers in American education; Amos Kendall, leading member of Jackson's "Kitchen Cabinet"; Thomas Hart Benton, the senator who was called Old Bullion because of his support of hard currency; Supreme Court Justice Joseph Story; and the other prominent Americans depicted on this page.

John Randolph, the bitter and eccentric Virginia congressman

John C. Calhoun, who clashed with Jackson over nullification

Nicholas Biddle, whose National Bank was killed by Jackson

William Lloyd Garrison, the uncompromising abolitionist

Angelica Van Buren, the very beautiful White House hostess

Rush-Bagot Agreement	1817	*Tours Northern states*
First Seminole War	1818	
Convention of 1818 signed in London		
Bank panic	1819	
Florida ceded by Spain		
Missouri Compromise	1820	*Re-elected President*
	1822	*Vetoes Cumberland Road Bill*
Monroe Doctrine	1823	*Announces Monroe Doctrine*
John Quincy Adams elected President	1825	
	1826	*Becomes regent of University of Virginia*
	1829	*Elected chairman of Virginia Constitutional Convention*
	1831	*Dies July 4*

BIOGRAPHICAL FACTS

BIRTH: Westmoreland County, Va., April 28, 1758
ANCESTRY: Scotch
FATHER: Spence Monroe; d. 1774
FATHER'S OCCUPATION: Carpenter; farmer
MOTHER: Elizabeth Jones Monroe
BROTHERS: Andrew (d. 1826); Joseph Jones (d. 1824)
WIFE: Elizabeth Kortright; b. New York, N.Y., June 30, 1768; d. Oak Hill, Va., Sept. 23, 1830
MARRIAGE: New York, N.Y., Feb., 1786
CHILDREN: Eliza (1787–?); Maria Hester (1804–1850)
HOMES: Ash Lawn, Charlottesville, Va.; Oak Hill, Loudoun County, Va.
EDUCATION: Parson Campbell's school; College of William and Mary
RELIGIOUS AFFILIATION: Episcopalian
OCCUPATION BEFORE PRESIDENCY: Lawyer
MILITARY SERVICE: Officer in Third Virginia Regiment and Continental Army (1776–1779)
PRE-PRESIDENTIAL OFFICES: Military Commissioner for Southern Army; Rep. to Va. Legislature; Member of Governor Jefferson's Council; Rep. to Va. House of Delegates; Rep. to Continental Congress; Rep. to Va. Assembly; Rep. to U.S. Senate; Minister to France; Minister to England; Governor of Va.; Secretary of State; Secretary of War
AGE AT INAUGURATION: 58
OCCUPATION AFTER PRESIDENCY: Writer
DEATH: New York, N.Y., July 4, 1831
PLACE OF BURIAL: Hollywood Cemetery, Richmond

ELECTION OF 1816

CANDIDATES	ELECTORAL VOTE
James Monroe Democratic-Republican	183
Rufus King Federalist	34

FIRST ADMINISTRATION

INAUGURATION: March 4, 1817; the Capitol, Washington, D.C.
VICE PRESIDENT: Daniel D. Tompkins
SECRETARY OF STATE: John Quincy Adams
SECRETARY OF THE TREASURY: William Harris Crawford
SECRETARY OF WAR: John C. Calhoun
ATTORNEY GENERAL: Richard Rush; William Wirt (from Nov. 15, 1817)
POSTMASTER GENERAL: Return Jonathan Meigs, Jr.
SECRETARY OF THE NAVY: Benjamin Crowninshield; Smith Thompson (from Jan. 1, 1819)
FIFTEENTH CONGRESS (March 4, 1817–March 4, 1819):
Senate: 34 Democratic-Republicans; 10 Federalists
House: 141 Democratic-Republicans; 42 Federalists
SIXTEENTH CONGRESS (March 4, 1819–March 4, 1821):
Senate: 35 Democratic-Republicans; 7 Federalists
House: 156 Democratic-Republicans; 27 Federalists
STATES ADMITTED: Mississippi (1817); Illinois (1818); Alabama (1819); Maine (1820)
END OF PRESIDENTIAL TERM: March 4, 1821

ELECTION OF 1820

CANDIDATES	ELECTORAL VOTE
James Monroe Democratic-Republican	231
John Quincy Adams Independent-Republican	1

SECOND ADMINISTRATION

INAUGURATION: March 5, 1821; House of Representatives, Washington, D.C.
VICE PRESIDENT: Daniel D. Tompkins
SECRETARY OF STATE: John Quincy Adams
SECRETARY OF THE TREASURY: William H. Crawford
SECRETARY OF WAR: John C. Calhoun
ATTORNEY GENERAL: William Wirt
POSTMASTER GENERAL: Return Jonathan Meigs, Jr.; John McLean (from July 1, 1823)
SECRETARY OF THE NAVY: Smith Thompson; Samuel L. Southard (from Sept. 16, 1823)
SUPREME COURT APPOINTMENT: Smith Thompson (1823)
SEVENTEENTH CONGRESS (March 4, 1821–March 4, 1823):
Senate: 44 Democratic-Republicans; 4 Federalists
House: 158 Democratic-Republicans; 25 Federalists
EIGHTEENTH CONGRESS (March 4, 1823–March 4, 1825):
Senate: 44 Democratic-Republicans; 4 Federalists
House: 187 Democratic-Republicans; 26 Federalists
STATE ADMITTED: Missouri (1821)
END OF PRESIDENTIAL TERM: March 4, 1825